ENGLISH LANGUAGE PEDAGOGY

ENGLISH LANGUAGE PEDAGOGY

Dr N. Devanki

KALPAZ

ISBN: 978-93-5128-111-5

Price: ₹ 690/-

Published by

Kalpaz Publications
C-30, Satyawati Nagar,
Delhi – 110052
E-mail: kalpaz@hotmail.com
Ph.: 9212142040

Laser Typesetting: Lucky Graphic, Delhi
Printed at: G. Print Process, Delhi

Cataloguing in Publication Data—DK

Courtesy: D.K. Agencies (P) Ltd. <docinfo@dkagencies.com>

Devanki, N., author.

English language pedagogy / N. Devanki.

pages cm

ISBN 9789351281115

1. English language—Study and teaching—India.

2. English language—Study and teaching (Secondary)—India. I. Title.

DDC 428.0071054 23

Contents

Preface

The 21st century beckoning with new science and technologies, offering ever expanding vistas of borderless world, challenging human intellect, imagination, initiative and ingenuity to explore, to protect, to adventure and thereby make waves. Teachers have to take up this challenge for preparing 21st century 'digital native' generation. Success in to the arena of quality education depends largely on teachers and their level of skills and competencies. Appropriate pedagogical training would benefit everyone engaged in the task of teaching. Hence, the trainee is expecting to attain a certain level of proficiency in teaching English. The book thoroughly discusses and provides adequate information to help the student to understand the implementations of each item for teaching/learning of English, especially at the secondary level. In this book entitled *English Language Pedagogy*, author has traced the latest innovations in the field of English Language. The basic purpose of writing the book is to provide a comprehensive matter of contents and methods of teaching English. It will help immensely to prospective teachers of English. It is also meant for Teacher working in Teachers Training colleges, B.Ed., Student Teachers, Teacher Educators, Public too. Hence, this book, "A Work of Worth", and "Ready to Refer".

Unit – I
Language Teaching

I. Language

"Language is a purely human and non-instinctive method of communicating ideas, emotions and desires by means of a system of voluntary produced symbols. These symbols are in the first instance auditory and they are produced by the so-called 'Organ of Speech'. There is no discernible instinctive basis for human speech as such, however, much instinctive tendencies, motor and other, may give a predetermined range or mould to linguistic expression. Such human or animal communication, if 'Communication' it may be called, as is brought about by involuntary, instinctive cries is not, in out sense language at all".

Man alone uses languages for communication. As Dwight Bolinger says, "Language is species-specific. It is unique humanly trait, shared by the cultures, so diverse and by individuals physically and mentally so unlike one another".

"Language is the set of human habits, the purpose of which is to give expression to human thoughts and feelings especially to impart them to others".

"Language is the set of arbitrary vocal symbols by means of which a social group communicate".

Language is a means of communicating thoughts and feelings though not the only means.

II. Nature of Language

If we look at the definition of language as given by a scholar, "Language is a learned arbitrary system of vocal symbols by means of which human beings interact and communicate in terms of their common cultural experiences".

From this definition we can find following things about the nature of language.

(1) Language is learnt : The child knows no language and he learns it over a long period of time. He beings learning of language by making various isolated sounds like Tha-Tha, Pa-Pa. Finally, he acquires the speech sounds of his group by imitation. He also learns grammatical constructions of the language by imitation.

(2) Language is a system : Just as various systems of our body (e.g., digestive system, respiratory system, circulation system) thought different yet work in co-ordination, similarly the system of language functions through sounds, words and structures. These are integrated and form the language.

(3) Arbitrariness of language : It is not essential to have any relationship between the word and the object for which it is spoken. We use different words for the same object in different languages e.g., Newspaper in English, *Samachar Patra* in Hindi, Library in English, *Pustakalaya* in Hindi etc.

(4) System and symbols : The symbols of a language are its words. For better functioning of a language it is essential that both speaker and listener know the words. Each word has a definite sound and a definite meaning. For communicating it is essential to attach a meaning to each sound.

(5) Language symbols are vocal : The word language has its origin in the Latin word 'Lingua' meaning 'which is produced with the tongue'. Language is basically a speech. Writing is graphical representation of speech. Many language exist only in spoken form, they do not have any written form.

(6) Language is based on common cultural experience : Every language is a product of particular society and culture. "Human language is transmitted from one individual to another not by physical inheritance, but by learning". It has meaning only in relation to a particular culture and society. We do not find two exactly equal words in any two languages. This is so because cultures are different.

(7) Language changes : Every language is a living language. The language is constantly changing and developing according to the needs of the speaker. New words are borrowed and absorbed in a language from time to time.

III. Functions of Language

The importance of language in the life of man cannot be over-emphasised. We cannot imagine a society without language. Language is the basis of human progress. It is the flesh and blood of human culture. Without language, civilisation could hardly even have begun and certainly could never have attained its higher forms.

Language is social, and we are constantly involved in the process of social interaction which it makes possible. Language is the means of social control. Human beings co-operate with one another through meaningful noises (spoken words) and scratches (written words).

There are three major functions of language :

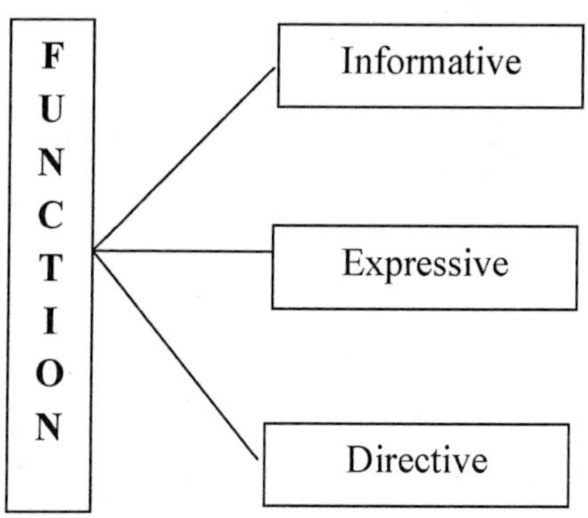

Informative function: Informative function is to communicate information. A geography teacher can give information about the Astronomy. A science teacher can give information about Ecology and Anatomy of Human. A history teacher can give information about the great personalities like Gandhi, Nehru, etc. Here, we make use of the language for communication.

Expressive function: Feelings, emotions and attitudes are also expressed through language. For example, in the lines of Mary Dobson in his poem, 'The Taj Mahal' that in life so long-time parted. Death no longer can divide. Here, the poet expressing his feelings not conveying any information.

Directive function: It is used to cause action. If the teacher commands the students to read a particular prose or poetry piece, it is not to communicate any information or to kindle any feeling or emotion by to cause action. Thus, the third function of a language is directive.

IV. Characteristics of Language

1. **Language is a system:** Language is a system like that of the human body. While the system of the body functions through various organs such as the heart, lungs, etc., the system of language functions through three important constituents, e.g., the sound, the structures and the words. There cannot be any utterance without making use of sounds, structures or vocabulary. Consider the sentence: Lalith played football. It consists of various sounds, i.e. (Lalid p, l, ei, d; f, u, t, b): (1) It follows a particular structure, i.e., subject, verb, object, and it makes use of certain words Lalith played, football.

In fact, language is a system of phonological, grammatical and lexical systems. The whole system of language cannot be taught whatever the number of years devoted to its study. So, the principle that language is a system stresses the importance of selection and graduation of language material. It is because of this reason that in structural approach, the structures and vocabulary items are carefully selected and graded.

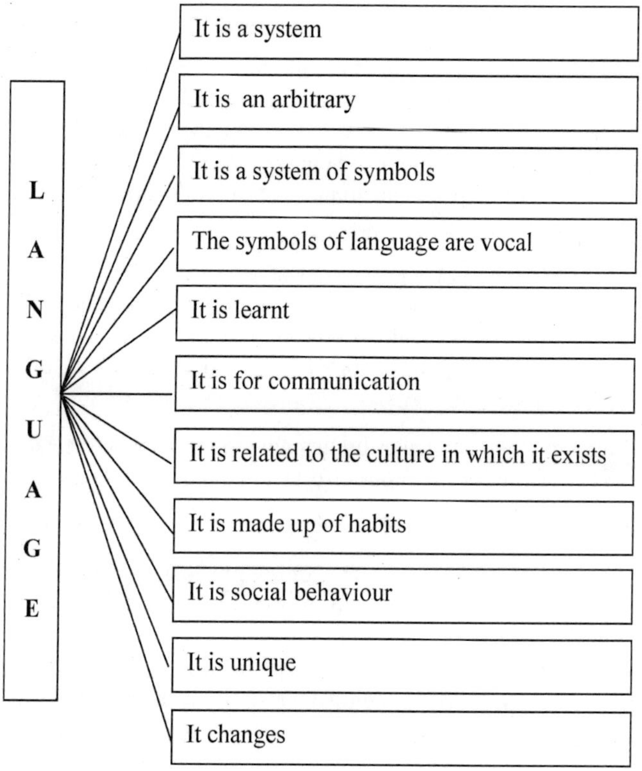

2. **Arbitrary system:** There is no relationship between a particular symbol, and the object denoted by it. For example, why do we call a particular object 'tree' or another object 'stone'? There is no relationship between the symbol 'tree' and the object denoted by it. The same is true in the case of 'stone' or other items of vocabulary. It is a matter of convention. Once the convention is set, it is not for the individual to break it. The same is true of question and answer forms. Why is it that, "Is this a tree?" is a question, and "This is a tree", a statement. It is also a matter of convention.

3. **A system of symbols:** Symbols are representations of things rather than the things themselves. The word 'boy' is not a 'boy'. It stands for a 'boy'. Language functions best only when the symbols are known to the speaker and the listener, the writer and the reader.

4. **Vocal symbols:** Languages uses vocal symbols which are made up of speech sounds. These sounds are produced by human beings through various movements of the vocal organs. Language is primarily speech; writing is only secondary. A language lives on the tongues of the people. This principle stresses the importance of oral work in teaching a language.

5. **Learned activity:** Language is a learned activity. It does not come automatically, as walking does. The child is not born with the skill of speaking. He has to acquire it after his born. If a child were to be isolated from society or brought up in the company of deaf people, he would not be able to pick up any language.

Children pick up languages by listening to their parents, relatives and friends. They put in strenuous efforts to learn their mother tongue.

Since language is a learned activity, we have to teach it properly.

6. **For communication:** The chief purpose of language is communication. We use language to inform others, to ask them to do certain things or to express our feelings or emotions. For this purpose, it is important that we acquire the right type of pronunciation which is intelligible to others. Teachers should, therefore, pay attention to correct speech on the part of students.

7. **Related to the culture in which it exists:** A language is the product of a particular society and culture. It has meaning only in relation to that society and culture. The Eskimos, for example, have so many different words in their language for 'snow'. It is because 'snow' plays an important role in their lives. But other languages do not have that number of words for 'snow'. In England, to ask a person about his salary is considered ill-mannered, but it is not so in India. The way of greeting, saying thanks etc., are different in different countries. It is because of cultural differences.

While learning a foreign language, a person does not only learn that particular language, but he also gets ample scope to be acquainted with the culture of the people whose language he is learning. The cultural aim of teaching a language cannot be ignored.

8. **Made up of habits:** According to Jesperson, "Language is a set of human habits, the purpose of which is to give expression to thoughts and feelings". The system of language is to be mastered at the habit level. When a person speaks his mother tongue, he does not consider the position of the various speech organs while make meaningful noise. Nor does he think of the ways in which he is putting various words to form sentences. It is because speaking has become a matter of habit with him. No person can be said to have learnt a language unless he masters it at the habit level. The student should be provided intensive practice in use of language. The teacher provides opportunities to the students to use the language.

9. **Social behaviour:** The features of language are not inherited in the biological sense, that is, heredity does not predispose a person to learn one language more easily than another. Language is social behaviour. A child picks up the language of his environment. If a child born in Tamil Nadu is brought up in London, he will pick up English, but if he is taken away to Moscow, he will learn Russian.

10. **Unique:** Each language is unique. No two languages have the same sound, grammatical or lexical systems. All languages differ in these respects. So, fresh efforts have to be made to learn a language.

11. **Dynamic**: Language is not static. A living language, like human beings, changes. If we study the history of any language, we shall notice the numerous changes that have taken place in it over the years.

V. Principles of Language Teaching

1. **Naturalness:** The mother-tongue is learnt more easily because a natural environment exists for learning it. It is spoken in family, and in neighbourhood. But this is not true for a foreign language. The child encounters with a foreign language in his class for about six periods a week, and so it becomes difficult for him to learn it. An effort can be made to provide the child with a natural environment for learning this foreign language. For this following points are important:

(i) Talking to the student in foreign language in the class, playground etc.

(ii) Encouraging students to converse only in this language.

(iii) Arranging for group discussion.

2. **Exposure:** A child learns his mother-tongue more rapidly, because he is exposed to it. As it is spoken around him, so he listens to it, and then he tries to speak it. For teaching foreign language, teacher should try to expose students to an environment loaded with the foreign language. For this he can take the following steps:

(i) Distribute pamphlets in foreign language.

(ii) Form a foreign language speaking club in the school.

(iii) Display charts with slogans written in English on walls etc.

(iv) Show slides in English.

(v) Take students to watch English movies.

(vi) Use mother-tongue in classroom be minimised to give students maximum exposure to English.

(vii) He can also make use of the technique of 'advance organiser'. For this, he should write some sentences on the blackboard before the students enter the class. When they come they will interestingly read that has been written on the blackboard.

3. **Habit formation:** Language learning is a skill like learning cycling, swimming, etc. As the instrument of all subjects, language learning should be automatic i.e., a habit. Language should be learnt to the point that little or no effort is made to speak it.

As Palmer says, "Language learning is essentially a habit-forming process, a process during which we acquire new habits". Thompson and Walt call it "unreflective right utterance".

In the learning of mother-tongue, we form speech habits. In learning a foreign language, speech habits are to be formed consciously. As indicated by Bruce Pattison, Habit has to be established; the operation of the system has to become fairly automatic".

Besides speech habits, a language learner has to form habits of reading and writing.

Following habits should be formulated in students:

(i) Listening to sounds and distinguishing between sounds,

(ii) Speaking with proper intonation and accent,

(iii) Imitating,

(iv) Repeating,

(v) Spelling,

(vi) Reading aloud with exact articulation,

(vii) Silent reading,

(viii) Using correct-grammar,

(ix) Using words in their proper context,

(x) Correct pronunciation,

(xi) Consulting dictionary,

(xii) Going to library,

(xiii) Reading newspapers, journals, story-books etc.

4. **Mother-tongue:** In his book *Understanding English*, Roberts Paul writes, "When we learnt first language, we face the universe directly and learn to clothe it with speech; when we learn a second language, we tend to filter the universe through the language already known". So, one can use mother-tongue in teaching a second language. To quote P. Gurrey, "the teaching of mother-tongue and the teaching of a foreign language can support and assist each other".

5. **Proper order:** Natural order of learning is made up of learning the four basic language skills: Listening, speaking, reading and writing. The classical order involved in teaching these skills is the following:

(i) Understanding (listening),

(ii) Speaking,

(iii) Reading, and

(iv) Writing.

J.A. Bright found by an experiment that reading becomes easy when writing is learnt before reading. Because in this way, associations between symbols and sounds can be made.

Proper proportion: In the words of Palmer, "It simply means that all items in the whole range of the subject and aspects must receive an appropriate degree of attention, so that the students' knowledge of them may ultimately form a harmonious whole". While teaching a language due and equal emphasis should be on each aspect. No skill should be over emphasised or neglected.

Passive and Active Vocabulary: There are two kinds of vocabulary.

Passive Vocabulary: It consists of those words which are recognised, and understood but seldom used in speaking and writing.

Active Vocabulary: It consists of those words which are understood and constantly used by the learner while speaking and writing.

Teacher should make a conscious effort to bring the words from passive vocabulary to active vocabulary of the child.

Motivation: Motivation plays very important role in learning a language. It is the core of learning. To motivate the student to learn a foreign language is an uphill task as there is no internal force for learning this language. Therefore, special techniques are required to motivate students to learning the foreign language. These are following:

(i) **Arousing techniques:** These include techniques that arouses students from a state of sleepiness, inducing anxiety, frustration, curiosity are of such techniques.

(ii) **Expectancy techniques:** There should be clear-cut goal to achieve, and an expectancy to achieve them, it is desirable for teachers to formulate clear-cut goals before students.

(iii) **Incentive techniques:** In this category, these are included techniques such as prize, praise, punishment, and completion etc.

Selection: As only limited things can be taught within a limited period, so the teaching matter has to be selected. Following points be kept in mind while selecting the teaching matter:

(i) **Frequency**: Those words or sentences should be selected which have a high frequency of occurrence (which are used a larger number of times), or which are frequently used, e.g. note, pencil, and pen.

(ii) **Range**: Every word has its range which shows the number of situations in which a word can be used. For example, consider the word 'star' and 'have' 'star' can be used only in one situation whereas 'have' can be used in three situations:

(a) They have studied the lessons.

(b) Have these cassettes.

(c) They have three cameras.

Thus, 'star' has a short-range whereas 'have' has a long-range. For teaching, select the word having a long-range.

(iii) **Availability:** Words convenient to teach and useful should be selected. The teacher as to see if the word is convenient to teach, as chalk, chair, board, etc., because of their availability in the classroom. He has to select the word as useful as TV, Mixie, Fan etc., because of their indispensable availability in house.

(iv) **Coverage:** Coverage refers to a word capacity to display the number of words, e.g., the word 'garden' has a capacity to display plant, tree, flower, and fruit, etc. Words which have more covering capacity should be selected.

(v) **Teachability:** While making a selection for teaching one should prefer those words which can be taught easily by making use of various devices. Words differ in teachability. One can easily choose the word 'apple' by showing an apple or by sketching an apple even by showing a picture of an apple. However, it is difficult to teach the words, 'Sympathy', 'Love', etc.

(vi) **Learnability:** It is desirable to teach things in accordance with the age of the child. A word that can be easily learnt by a class XII student may not be learnt so easily by a class VI student. While making a selection of matter to be taught the age of the student is kept in mind. Choice should be made keeping in mind the learnability of the students. W.R. Lee opines, "teach first those sentence-structures, the use of which can be made clear by means of visible action in the classroom".

(vii) **Gradation:** Practice alone enables the learner to acquire the habit of speaking the language. One of the important maxims of teaching is "proceed from simple to difficult" and "from more useful to less useful". Selected words and structures are put in suitable order for teaching them. This is called gradation. There are two principles which come under gradation principles:

(viii) **Principle of grouping:** According to it the material selected is grouped on the basis of sound, situation, sentence-structure, and meaning. It helps to make the process of learning easier. If the material is grouped on the basis of sound, it is called 'phonetic grouping', e.g. go, row, sow, toe, show, how, throw, etc. If the basis of grouping of words is situation then it is called 'lexical grouping', e.g. father, mother, brother, sister, etc. When the basis of grouping of teaching material is 'sentence-structure' then it is called 'grammatical'. If the material is grouped on the basis of meaning then it is called 'Semantic grouping'.

(ix) **Principle of sequencing:** The following three types of sequences help in the teaching material, and to decide which item should follow which one :

(a) *Grammatical sequence:* All suitable structures having subject, verb, and object should be taught first of all and only after this structures having subject – verb – object extension be taught, e.g., "I am going to Meerut" be taught first, and then only should we teach "I am going to Meerut to seek admission".

(b) *Lexical sequence:* It is concerned with the fact which word follows which, e.g. or follows either; nor follows neither, etc.

(c) *Semantic sequence:* Words of same or rather same meanings are taught one by one. For example:

(a) They all take meal.

(b) They take breakfast in the morning.

(c) They take lunch at noon, and

(d) They take dinner at night.

VI. Phonology

Emphasising the importance of speech Wren states, "There was speech in the world a long time before there was writing". To remember written symbols, it is always desirable to attach them with spoken symbols. Therefore, teaching a foreign language should start with hearing sounds and speaking the language. Beginning should be made with a speech lesson and in no case it should start from writing. Oral speech is the quickest way of learning a language. Thompson and Wyatt opine, book work and pen wait introduce passivity instead of activity, and work introduces activity".

Interest: According to Wren, "Lessons can be made interesting by utilising object and pictures, interesting to the class; by allowing all boys to do something as well as to say something; by giving fullest play….." the student teacher can make use of the following to arouse interest:

(i) Audio-visual aids – Linguophone, CD, OHP and LCD.

(ii) Relating the material to everyday life, and

(iii) Undertaking various activities such as speaking, reading, writing, etc.

Learning by doing: Written work, pronunciation, reading, spelling, writing, hearing are essential activities for foreign language learning. Students should be given a good practice of these processes.

Multiple line of approach: According to R.N. Safaya, "The term multiple line implies that one is to proceed simultaneously from many different points towards the one, and the same end". The teacher should adopt many approaches judiciously and rationally selected to reach the goal. Following approaches may be used:

(i) Social,

(ii) Functional,

(iii) Cultural,

(iv) Behavioural,

(v) Phonetic,

(vi) Situational, and

(vii) Structural.

Accuracy and Correctness: Accuracy means to make usage of right words. Only those words should be used which impart meaning for contexts. Following points may be remembered:

(i) The selection of word should be right,

(ii) Use of word should be economical, and

(iii) Expression should be impressive.

Correctness also implies the accuracy of pronunciation, intonation, spelling- structure and articulation. Thus, the teacher should be both accurate and correct in the very beginning.

Storage: Knowledge can be stored in mind permanently, if it is gained through practical experience. A child can remember, 'Grapes' more if he has seen them. P.C. Wren says, "the first word of English should be names of things, and those things should be there before him as they are named. He must say "pen", "board" etc., and point to the things he names. For this, the teacher can make use of either the class-room material or can carry with him some handy material. This principle be also kept in mind while teaching adjectives, pronouns, prepositions, conjunction, verbs, and adverbs, etc.

Correlation with life: Teacher should correlate the subject-matter to life, customs, traditions, peculiarities and characteristics of the society to which the student belongs. This will make teaching more meaningful and learning shall be transferred to real life situations.

Language aptitude: Carrol and Spoon have opined that language aptitude is needed for learning a language. The main components of language to be developed in students are as follows:

(i) Phonetic-coding or ability to code sounds in such a way that it can be remembered.

(ii) Ability to handle grammar.

(iii) Rote memorisation, and

(iv) Inferring linguistic rules, patterns, etc.

Imitation: Good speech is the result of imitating good models of speech provided by the teacher. For this purpose, the teacher can take help of various audio-visual aids such as tape-recorder, gramophone, etc. The learner should get good models of reading and writing.

An aim is a foreseen goal that gives direction to all activity. When we set out to do something unless we have the goal in our minds, we will not know in which direction we should proceed our aim in teaching English at the secondary school is to make our student acquire a mastery over the basic skills of English-listening, speaking, reading and writing. We begin teaching English at the third standard. By the time, the pupil leaves the tenth standard our aim will have to be achieved. An aim is reached by moving along with several smaller steps taken towards our goals. Each such step is called an objective. Objective is a tiny component of the aim. We have to reach out aims in eight years.

An individual may need English for a variety of purposes competence in English may help him to secure a job locally and abroad, read useful and interesting books in English for information or for pleasure. The community too needs people with proficiency in English for a number of reasons for: (a) manning the government departments; (b) for representing the nation in international forums; (c) for unifying people living in different regions, and speaking different languages, and for (d) promoting international understanding. The aims of learning and teaching English may thus be vocational, linguistic, literary, cultural, and integrative and so on. The aim of teaching English in schools should be utilitarian as well as linguistic. To put it differently, the aims of teaching English in schools is to give the pupils a basic all-round command of English.

VII. First Language

Learning Conditions of L1 and L2

There is a world of difference between the child learning or rather acquiring his native language and the adult acquiring a foreign language. In our understanding of the acquisition process of a language these two understanding may be considered types: the learning of L1, i.e. one or more languages learned in the family environment, in absolutely congenial circumstances without the cumbersome activities of the classroom. In India, especially, it is a usual phenomenon that a child is required to learn more than one language as its first language without any one conspicuously dominating the others. There are several possible variations among what we may call: the mother-tongue, i.e., the language of the parents, (it also happens that the parents belongs to different linguistic communities), the local language, the regional language, and the national language. It happens that a child from the very beginning comes in touch with and is compelled to learn quite a few of these varieties of language. It is not possible for us to differentiate the learning processes of those languages as each of these has similar or the same learning environment. Therefore, in the present work by L1 we mean all the languages mentioned above, i.e. the set of languages that a child picks up before the school-going age.

Communication is a key to successful second language learning; you will centre attention on non-verbal systems and cues. If you perceive language as a phenomenon that can be dismantled into thousands of discrete pieces and those pieces programmatically taught one by one, you will attend carefully to an understanding of the separability of the forms of languages. There are few right and wrong answers to questions about language. Truth is multifaceted and usually lies in an undecipherable gray area.

Many other more particular aspects will have to be understood in the context of the teacher's training programme in a particular language, in which specialised training in linguistics is obviously recommended along with a careful analysis of the foreign language itself.

A second language (L2) is any language learned after the first language or mother tongue (L1) some languages, often called auxiliary languages, is used primarily as second languages or lingua francas.

It is quite possible that the first language a person learns may no longer be their dominant language, that is, the one he or she uses most or the one with which he or she is most comfortable in. For example, the Canadian census defines first language for its purposes as "the first language learned in childhood and still spoken", recognising that for some, the earliest language may be lost, a process known as language attrition. This can happen when young children move, with or without their family (because of immigration or international adoption), to a new language environment.

Age

According to some researchers, the defining difference between a first language (L1) and a second language (L2) is the age at which the language was learned. For example, linguist Eric Lenneberg used second language to mean a language consciously acquired or used by its speaker after puberty. In most cases, people never achieve the same level of fluency and comprehension in their second languages as in their first language. These views are closely associated with the Critical Period Hypothesis.

In acquiring an L2, Hyltenstam (1992), found that around the age of six and seven seemed to be cut-off point for bilinguals to achieve native-like proficiency. After that age L2, learners could get near-native-like-ness but their language would, while consisting of very few actual errors, have enough errors that would set them apart from the L1 group. The inability of some of the subjects to achieve native-like proficiency must be seen in relation to the age of onset (AO). "The age of six or eight does seem to be an important period in distinguishing between near-native and native-like ultimate attainment.... More specifically, it may be suggested that AO interacts with frequency and intensity of language use" (Hyltenstam, 1992, p. 364).

Later, Hyltenstam and Abrahamsson (2003), modified their age cut-offs to argue that after childhood, in general, it becomes more and more difficult to acquire native-likeness, but that there is no cut-off point in particular. Furthermore, they discuss a number of cases where a native-like L2 was acquired during adulthood.

Speed

Acquiring a second language can be a life-long learning process for many. Despite persistent efforts, most learners of a second language will never become hilly native-like in it, although with practice considerable fluency can be achieved. However, children by around the age of five have more or less mastered their first language, with the exception of vocabulary and a few grammatical structures.

Stages

Acquiring a second language occurs in systematic stages. Much evidence has been gathered to show that basic sounds, vocabulary, negating phrases, forming questions, using relative clauses, and so on are developed. This development is independent from input (we do not hear not read language in this order), independent from learning situation (in the classroom or on the street), and is generally applicable across a spectrum of learners (from different language backgrounds). This is similar to the learning stages that babies go through when acquiring the first language: babbling (bababa), vocabulary (milk then later milk drink), negation (no play), question forming (where she go), and so on.

Correction

Error correction does not seem to have a direct influence on learning a second language. Instruction may affect the rate of learning, but the stages remain the same. Adolescents and adults, who know the rule, are faster than those who do not in the first language, children do not respond to systematic correction. Furthermore, children who have limited input still acquire the first language.

Depth of knowledge

Learners in the first or second language have knowledge that goes beyond the input they received, in other words, the whole is greater than the parts. Learners of a language are able to construct correct utterances (e.g., phrases, sentences, and questions) that they have never seen or heard before.

Success

Success in language learning can be measured in two ways: likelihood and quality. First language learners will be successful in both measurements. It is inevitable that all first language learners will learn a first language with few exceptions, they will be fully successful. For second language learners, success is not guaranteed. For one, learners may become fossilised or stuck as it were with ungrammatical items. (Fossilisation occurs when language errors become a permanent feature. See Canale and Swain (1980), Johnson (1992), Selinker (1972), and Selinker and Lamendela (1978)). The difference between learners may be significant. Finally, as noted elsewhere, L2 learners rarely achieve complete native-like control of the second language.

VIII. Multilingual Context of India

Multilinguism in India is a challenging and stimulating study of the nature and structure of multilinguism in the Indian sub-continent. India, with 1652 mother tongues, between 200 and 700 languages belonging to four language families, written in ten major script systems, and a host of minor ones, represents multilingualism unparalleled in the democratic world. With a multitude of communities, its multilingualism matches its pluriculturalism.

The articles in this book discuss sociology, psychology, pedagogy and demographic aspects of multilingualism. They bring out some of the salient problems of literacy in a multilingual world and give a language planning perspective. The volume ends with a discussion on language, and social identity. In a multilingual country like India, many languages are mutually supportive and complement one another. Identities are layered and larger identities encompass the smaller ones without absorbing them. The unique social document will appeal equally to linguists, social scientists and educators, while offering new insights to all those interested in differences among social groups and how communication in different settings unites them. It will enable the reader to enter into the classroom, a tribal home, and contexts in which multilingual discourses take place, in order to understand the many deeply ingrained language habits, values, and attitudes of India".

IX. Three-language Formula

In order to provide facilities for teaching a minority language or mother tongue, State Education Ministers evolved a scheme in 1949. Subsequently, the Union Education Ministry in consultation with States formulated a Three-Language Formula. This formula as enunciated in the National Policy Resolution of 1968 and reiterated in the National Policy on Education 1986 provides Hindi, English and Modern Indian language (preferably one of the southern languages) in the Hindi speaking states and Hindi.

English and the regional language in non-Hindi speaking states. This formula has created many difficulties for Urdu speakers. The major grievance of Urdu speaking linguistic minority is that their children have been denied the facility of mother tongue instruction. The result is that large number of children of Urdu speakers are learning the regional language instead of the mother tongue as the first language. Accordingly, the Gujral Committee recommended the following modified form of three-language formula:

(i) In Hindi speaking states:

- (a) Hindi (with Sanskrit as part of the composite course);
- (b) Urdu or any other modern Indian language excluding (a), and
- (c) English or any other modern European language.

(ii) In non-Hindi speaking states:

- (a) Regional language;
- (b) Hindi;
- (c) Urdu or any other modern Indian language excluding (a) and (b); and
- (d) English or any other modern European language (4.240).

The three language formula, at present in vogue in Andhra Pradesh with a degree of success, may also be adopted as an alternative by the non-Hindi speaking states for Urdu speaking population. The formula is:

- (a) Urdu and Hindi (a composite course);
- (b) Regional language;
- (c) English or any other modern European language (4.241).

The Gujral Committee felt that in any formula that is worked out, it should be ensured that students are able to study their mother tongue as well as the official language of the State.

The State-wise position of the languages and the stages:

X. Medium of Instruction

1. That the Federal languages to be developed through the assimilation of words from various sources, and the retention of words which have already entered into Indian languages from different sources, thereby avoiding the dangers of exclusiveness.
2. The international technical and scientific terminology must be adopted, the borrowed words be properly assimilated, their pronunciation be adopted to the phonetic system of the Indian language and their spelling fixed in accordance with the second symbols of Indian scripts.
3. That for the medium of instruction for higher education English be replaced as early as practicable by an Indian language which cannot be Sanskrit on account of vital difficulties.
4. That (i) pupils at the higher secondary and University stages be made conversant with three languages the regional languages, the Federal language and English (the last one in order to acquire the ability to read book in English) and (i) Higher education be imparted through the instrumentality of the regional language with the option to use the Federal language as the medium of instruction either for some subjects or for all the subjects.
5. That for the Federal language one script, Devnagari, be employed and some of its defects be removed.
6. That immediate step should be taken for developing the Federal and Regional languages.
   (i) A board consisting of scientific and linguists be appointed to prepare a scientific vocabulary of words which will be common to all Indian languages and also to arrange for the preparation of books in different sciences to be rendered into all Indian languages.
   (ii) Provincial governments to be required to take steps to introduce the teaching of Federal in all of Higher Secondary school, in degree colleges and in universities.

7. The English be studied in high schools and in the universities in order that we may keep in touch with the living stream of ever-growing knowledge.

XI. Psychology of Language Learning

In his classic work on the conditions of learning, the Robert Gagne aptly demonstrated the importance of identifying a number of different types of learning which all human use. Types of learning vary according to the content and subject matter to be learned. But the complex task such as language learning involves every one of Gagne's type of learning from simple signal learning to problem solving. Gagne identified eight types of learning.

(i) **Signal learning :** The individual learns to make a general diffuse response to a signal. This is the classical conditional response of Pavlov.

(ii) **Stimulus response learning :** The teacher acquires a precise response to a discriminated operant sometimes called instrumental response.

(iii) **Chaining :** What is acquired is a chain of two or more stimulus response connections. The conditions for such learning have also been described by skinner.

XII. Recommendation in NPE

1. A National Policy on Education is formulated in 1968, largely to implement the Kothari Commission Report. It was noted at regional languages which were used as media of instruction should be made the media at college level too. The fact that a large number of English medium schools were flourishing all over the country has been side-tracked by the policy-makers. The NPE 1968 recommended the strengthening of Hindi as a link language and English as language of science and technology.

2. The next stage in policy-making was the National Policy on Education (NPE 1986), and the Programme of Action (POA) which reiterated the earlier view on strengthening languages. NPE 1986, asked for the setting up of rural schools, colleges and universities. The Navodaya Vidyalayas were set up under this plan.

3. The Acharya Rama Murti Committee (1986) had endorsed that the three-language formula had stood the test of time. They also emphasised the hours of study and levels of attainment in Hindi and English, irrespective of the duration of study. These competencies should be evolved and specified by the premier institutions (KHS CIEFL and CIIL) incharge of these subjects.

It is quite clear from these recommendations that nobody has said anything against English, and many people including policy-makers, administrators and parents even now feel that English teaching should be strengthened at all stages. There is an unmistakable public opinion that learning English voluntarily is for our own good. English and our own languages would naturally gain immensely by being learnt with different levels of competencies for different people.

4. Verbal association

Verbal association is the learning of chains that are verbal. Basically, the conditions resemble those for other (motor) chains. However, the presence of language in the human being makes this a special type because internal links may be selected from the individual previously learned repertoire of language.

5. Multiple discrimination

The individual learns to make a number of different identifying responses to many different stimuli which may resemble each other in physical appearance to a greater and lesser degree. Although, the learning of each stimulus response connection in a simple accordance, the connection tend to interface with one another.

6. Concept learning

The learner acquires the ability to make a common response to a class of stimuli even though the individual members of that class may differ widely from each other. The learner is able to make a response that identities and entire class of objects and events.

7. Principle learning

In simple terms, a principle is a chain of two or more concepts. The main function is to organise behaviour and experience. In Ausubel's terminology, a principle is a "sustained", a cluster of related concepts.

8. Problem solving

Problem solving is a kind of learning that requires the internal events usually referred to as "thinking" previously acquired concepts and principles are combined in a conscious focus on an unresolved or ambiguous set of events.

XIII. Language – the primary need of the child

There is a proverb in English, necessity is the mother of invention. "Language is such expression and communication to or from human beings by means of speech and hearing, the sounds uttered or heard, being so combined in systems involved, conventionalised and recognised by common usage in a given community that they are mutually intelligible to all, approximately normal members thereof".

L.H. Gray: Foundation of Language

So, it is not a surprising fact that every human child is able to learn a language, which is foreign to the child during the first four to five years of life. The new-born baby learns not only to understand the mother-tongue, but to speak it with fluency and accuracy. During this period, his intellect is comparatively weak. His mind is least equipped with language abilities and his reasoning powers immature. Then, what, is the motivating force which renders this tremendous amounting of learning so efficiently? What is the process? The force is provided by the gregarious impulse – the necessity to participate in the ideas, feeling and actions of the mother, the father and the family circle. His social participation enriches the mind with experiences. The mind thus developed and enriched has got something to say and he says it somehow. The words or sounds available in the environment are readily picked up, for use and reuse. Imitation and invention go a long way in language learning. This is the process.

Educational Implications

The process is mainly imitative and wholly conscious under normal conditions. The act of imitating the elders, when frequently repeated, takes the form of a habit. But his imitative and habitual acts are not wholly reproductive. He constructs his own structures and sentences though grammatically wrong, and coins his own words and phrased to explain new situations. Yet before long, without the knowledge of grammar, he learns to speak correct sentences and without the use of dictionary he acquires right meanings of words. He may learn to speak incorrectly because of the defective models of speech in the family, but the meanings of words he acquires are as a rule correct. Under special demands, it becomes a conscious process, a process of language communication. The problems encountered by children in this process had attracted attention of the Research Wing of Bombay Municipal Corporation in 1970, and sought to improve and develop language communication skill of children by establishing firm and good habits in speech.

Language – as Medium of Growth

The history of the development and language of the race is the history of the growth of intelligence. Man's superiority over other animals is mainly due to language. Speech is essentially a human faculty. It is an extremely complicated mental phenomenon, involving not merely the functioning of neuro-motor apparatus for uttering meaningful sounds, i.e., vocal symbols for things and actions; the auditory recognition of the spoken words as speech symbols; the interpretation of visual impressions including signs, pictorial or graphical symbols, gestures etc., but also an elaborate mental mechanism of association which, ender possible the syntactic combination of auditory symbols which make human language.

Educational Implication

Human language has kept pace with the growth of civilisation. So also it keeps pace with the growth of the individual man. In the beginning the individual deals only with the concrete in his infancy and early childhood. Then he learns to deal with abstract ideas. Education to some extent is the growth of these language habits and this growth can be measured. Nowadays, the best single measure of the intelligence of an educand or a citizen is the size of the vocabulary. This is the age of speech machines; telephone, gramophone, radio, television and talkie have increased and enlarged the powers and functions of the language on the world stage. Human relations and associations have cut across the regional barriers, and the modern civilised man must be prepared to maintain the links of international communication. According to Goethe, "he who knows no foreign language knows nothing of his own". Language is to the intellect what body is to the soul. Growth is the characteristic of life. Growth takes place by means of habit formation. So, the intellectual growth is shaped by the language habit from the very beginning when the child depends upon his mother, father, teacher and society for the formation of such habits. The mother-tongue habits are further utilised in learning a second language or a foreign language.

Language and Social Life

Language is the essential requirement of all human co-operative work. According to Ben Johnson, 'speech is the instrument of society'. It is used not only for giving and receiving information but also for joining man to man by way of greetings, conversations, enquiries, co-operation and discussion. The definition of language as means of communication of thoughts is nowadays considered as a partial truth; more useful definition is that language is a means of social control. The author is writing a book and this work of writing involves the work of many people. His ideas are derived through language from several sources from teachers, from books, magazines and newspapers, from discussions and discourses, and a number of other sources. After the writing-work is over, the book will entail co-operation of many people in printing, binding, publishing and selling. The book will receive social co-operation, if its language is befitting to the social context, and is powerful enough to stimulate the imagination readers. If the words of the author come to mean less and less to the reader, his eyes will glaze over the lines, breaking down his imagination and dissociating the mind from full consciousness, and he will gradually stop participating in the discussions here. Ideas emerge and crystallise in the mind by means of language. The aim of language teacher is to seek action-action which gives rise to speech. The purpose of language teacher is to train in speech. Social action fertilises the ground in which abilities and skills connected with speech are developed. The language teacher not only makes his pupils think and feel but he teaches them to act as well. He teaches the four arts, the four skills speaking, reading, writing and comprehension.

Educational Implications

In the class-room the imagination and the intellect of the pupils must help each other by establishing the normal social interplay of language. Work done in pairs or groups is more profitable and useful than the work done alone. Pupils may be asked to rehearse the dialogues, fluency exercise should be practiced in groups and composition exercises should be written in collaboration with other pupils, the stronger child helping the weaker child to produce better results. Thus, a habit of co-operative work and the knowledge that any sign of weakness brings sympathetic help not ridicule or scorn, will build up a workshop atmosphere in the classroom in which pupils participation and contribution to co-operative learning will increase and unhealthy rivalries will be discouraged. Pupils will develop a higher sense of responsibility on the general morale of the class will rise.

Language and Intellectual Traditions

Intellectual tradition is a very powerful factor in growth, development and maturity of the scholars at different levels of education, and in different branches of scholarship. Intellect assumes concrete form by means of language. It provides the medium through which the scholar makes his contact with the tradition, imbibes the spirit of that tradition through the medium of language. He learns to make use of language according to the intellectual tradition of the discipline. Thus, intellectual, tradition is the sum total of all intellectual influences ultimately determines his modes of thinking, speaking and writing. At higher levels, he masters that language in which the intellectual tradition of that branch of study is embodied. During the course of training, he acquires certain abilities of language which he frequently uses to express his ideas, to discuss and to elucidate the problems pertaining to the field of his specialisation. As such the role of language at higher level of education, and in the specialised fields of study is more than mere picking up information and knowledge. A true scholar must learn to participate in the intellectual traditions of the subject, and to get into grips with the fundamentals of the subject and to get into spirit of the tradition, feeling that he is a part of it. At this level, the scholar uses his own judgment to evaluate the traditions in order to make his own creative contribution to it. A scholar, who has, thus, participated in the traditions, who have achieved mastery over the medium (language) of thought and expression; and who has imbibed the spirit of the traditions, develops his own style embodying all the peculiarities may have temperamental differences; but due to the common intellectual tradition and a common language will have a kindred style; and an unmistakable community of spirit will be clearly visible in their creative works.

Educational Implications

Some people will put forth the argument that English being a more mature language, having a rich literary heritage, can be used most appropriately for any literary creative work. There is no doubt that English has a rich literature in the works of Shakespeare, Milton, Wordsworth, etc. But it is wrong to assume that in the academic disciplines English has achieved maturity of expression combined with an ease and originality in academic investigations and research, because of these masters. In fact, each academic discipline has its own traditions which in some cases go back to over a thousand years; but the literature in academic disciplines, mostly in the form of prose, is not even a century old. The two traditions are independent of each other. There is no doubt that academic traditions get much impetus from the already existing literary and poetic traditions. Indian languages can be used effectively for the expression of original thinking and research by cultivating and establishing new traditions in that academic discipline. From the point of view of creative writing nothing but original work and writing in Indian languages can improve the situation. Some of the talented scholars of high repute in the Indian academic world should be stimulated to contribute to the growth of academic traditions in one of the Indian languages or in Hindi. Unless our language or languages get a place in the deliberations, work, research and scholarship at the highest level, we cannot build the tradition. Without this, Indian languages will remain weak, and the scholars will continue to depend on English resulting into continued enslavement by the West.

As long as the scholars of repute employ English as their medium of expression, no substantial growth can take place in the indigenous academic traditions. The new Indian scholar continues to suffer from paucity of original thinking, because the use of English implies that the scholar should first grasp the fundamentals of the western intellectual tradition of which English is the main vehicle. When he is required to make an intellectual inquiry more and more in the Indian context he feels ill at ease.

Summary

Language is not merely the medium of instruction at all levels of education; it is the medium of growth. It provides capacity for preservation and communication of intellectual life. At higher level, language provides the medium of fresh and free thinking and research. In education, it is supposed to communicate knowledge, and in general life it is the instrument to pick up information. It is the primary need of the child, for self-expression..

The history of the development of language of the race is the history of the growth of intelligence. Man's superiority over other animals is mainly due to language. The mother-tongue habits are further utilised in learning a second language or a foreign language. It goes without saying that it is essential for all the human co-operative work and an important part of the society.

Intellect assumes concrete form by means of language hence the role of language at higher level of education and in the specialised fields of study is more than mere picking up information and knowledge.

Some people will put forth the argument that English being – a more mature language, having a rich literary heritage, can be used most appropriately for any literary creative work; but, as a matter of fact, Indian languages can also be used effectively for the expression of original thinking and research by cultivating and establishing new traditions in that academic discipline. As long as the scholars of repute employ English as their medium of expression, no substantial growth can take place in the indigenous academic traditions. Until and unless a man has full possession of language, the most amiable qualities of his nature shall have to lie uncultivated and buried.

The protagonists of English generally draw our attention to the fear that when English is driven out of India, we shall be cut off from the rest of the academic world. This does not mean that we shall always remain at the receiving end, and we shall never rise to a level high enough, where others will look to us for new ideas. Once the Indian languages and their scholars attain intellectual prestige and they start producing original work in Indian language or languages the barrier of language will not be felt so keenly. When the whole nation becomes alive enough mentally (it can never do so with English) it can participate easily in the intellectual march of the whole race.

Unit – II

Objective of Teaching

Teaching – Learning Strategies – Objectives of English Teaching – cognitive, affective and psychomotor levels.

Teaching methods – the grammar-translation, Direct, Dr West's, substitution, assignment, group, and play-way method.

Structural approach, situational approach, and communicative approach.

Teaching of prose, poetry, vocabulary, grammar, non-detail and composition.

I. Objective of Teaching English

Identification of Teaching Objectives

The teaching objectives are identified after analysing the content to be taught because teaching is a meaningful and purposeful activity. The teaching objectives are determined in the planning step. The teacher can identify his teaching objectives with the help of his knowledge and understanding of educational objectives.

Definition and Meaning of Educational Objectives

The objective is a statement or a form of category which suggests any kind of change. The objective has the following characteristics.

1. It provides the direction to the activity which is designed for achieving the ultimate goal.
2. It helps for the planned change.
3. It provides the basis for organising activities.

"The educational objectives imply the changes that we try to produce in the child".

The educational objectives are generally in the form of statement. These are broad and philosophical in nature. The teaching objectives are specific and psychological in nature. The teaching strategies and tactics are selected on the basis of teaching learning objectives. B.S. Bloom has given a very comprehensive definition of educational objectives.

1. Educational objectives,
2. Learning Experience, and
3. Change in behaviour.

B.S. Bloom believes that education is a tri-polar process

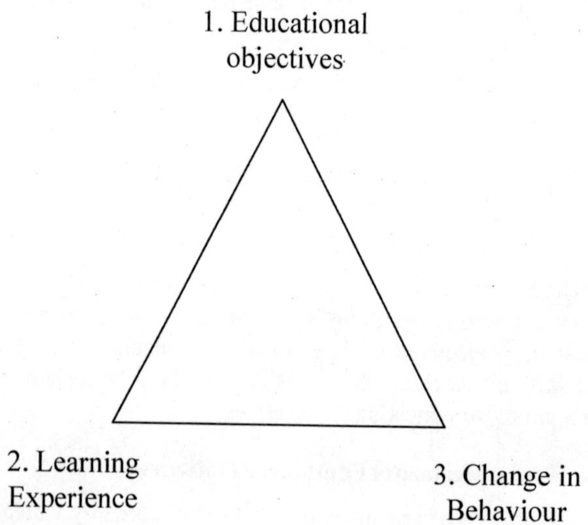

The learning experiences are provided by teaching activities to achieve educational objectives and change of behaviour is evaluated in terms of educational objectives. Thus, educational objectives are the basis for teaching activities and evaluation techniques.

The teaching objectives are achieved in terms of change of behaviour of learners. These are specific, direct and practical in nature. So, these are the most useful for teachers. B.S. Bloom has classified the learning objectives in three categories:

1. Cognitive objectives,
2. Affective objectives, and
3. Psycho-motor objectives.

II. Taxonomic Categories of Domains

Cognitive Domain	Affective Domain	Psycho-motor Domain
5. Evaluation	5. Organisation and Characterisation	6. Habit Formation
4,5. Analysis and Synthesis	4. Conceptualisation	4,5. Co-ordination and control
3. Application	3. Valuing	3. Manipulation
2. Comprehension	2. Responding	2. Imitation
1. Knowledge	1. Receiving	1. Impulsion

The above chart indicates that each domain consists of six categories. These categories are in a hierarchial order. The first is the pre-requisite of the second and first five categories are the pre-requisite of the last category.

An old educational oxiom states that 'growth occurs from within' and this inner-growth is demonstrated in the two taxonomies by the way in which they are internally related.

The following is the condensed version of educational objectives of cognitive domain.

Direction	***Category***
Low-level	1. *Knowledge*: (Remembering facts, terms and principles in the form that they were learned);
	(a) Knowledge of specifics; (i) Knowledge of terminology, (ii) Knowledge of specific facts, (b) *Knowledge of ways and means of dealing with specifics;* (i) Knowledge of convention, (ii) Knowledge of trends and sequences, (iii) Knowledge of classification and categories, (iv) Knowledge of criteria, (v) Knowledge of methodology, (c) Knowledge of universals and abstraction in a field; (i) Knowledge of principles and generalisations, (ii) Knowledge of theories and structures, 2. *Comprehension:* (Understanding material without necessarily relating it to other material); (a) Translation, (b) Interpretation, and (c) Extrapolation 3. *Application:* (Using generalisations or abstractions appropriately in concrete situations);
Medium-level	4. *Analysis* (Breakdown the material into its constituents situations); (a) Analysis of elements, (b) Analysis of relationship, and

	(c) Analysis of generalisational principles. 5. *Synthesis*: (Combining elements into new structure); (a) Production of unique communications, (b) Production of a plan or proposed set of operations, and (c) Derivation of a set of abstract relations.
High-level	*6. Evaluation:* (Judging the value of material for a specified purpose) (a) Judgement in terms of internal evidence, (b) Judgement in terms of external criteria.

Taxonomy of Affective Educational Objectives and Learning Outcomes

Krath who, *et.al.* (1964) have produced a hand-book and taxonomy designed to stimulate and systematise an assessment of objectives in the affective domain, as Bloom's Taxonomy has done in the cognitive area.

The correct answer of an affective question depends upon the person queried and response in social situations, but the correct answer of a cognitive question is the same for all respondents. Situational factors of the examiner and an assessment context have a more significant influence on the results for affective measures than they do for ability measures.

Condensed version of the taxonomy of educational objectives in an affective domain

Direction	*Category*
Low-level	1. *Receiving:* (Pay attention); (a) Awareness, (b) Willingness to receive, and (c) Controlled as selected attention.

	2. *Responding:* (Committed and actively attending); (a) Acquiscence in responding, (b) Willingness to respond, and (c) Satisfaction to response. 3. *Valuing*: (Concepts are seen to have worth); (a) Acceptance of a value, (b) Preference for a value, and (c) Commitment (conviction). 4. *Organisation:* (Construction of system of values); (a) Conceptualisation of a value, (b) Organisation of value system. 5. *Characterisation of complex values.* (Acceptance of value system); (a) Generalised set, (b) Characterisation.

Writing learning objectives in behavioural terms

The identification of objectives in terms of taxonomic categories does not specify the form of teaching, and learning activities. Therefore, it is essential to write these objectives in behavioural terms. The behavioural form of the objectives reveals the learning activities.

Mager's Approach of Writing Objectives

In Robert Mager's approach of writing the objectives following points are to be considered:

1. Firstly, identify the terminal behaviour by name; we can specify the kind of behaviour which will be accepted as evidence that the learner has achieved the objectives.
2. Secondly, try to further define the desired behaviour by describing the important conditions under which the behaviour will be expected to occur.

3. Thirdly, specify the criteria of acceptable performance by describing how the learner will must perform to be considered acceptable.

Although, the three statements are not always necessary, it is a very good rule of thumb for beginners that they must follow the layout exactly.

Miller's Approach of Writing Objectives

Robert Miller (1962) tackles the problem of writing objectives more the point of view of skill-analysis and according to him a clear objective should be preferably written in the following manner.

1. An indicator on which the activity, relevant-indication appear.
2. The indication or one which calls for a response.
3. The control objective is to be activated.
4. The activation or manipulation is to be made.
5. The indication of response should be adequate or feed-back.

Objectives of Teaching English

English language is taught as first language in most of the countries of the world. English language is considered a window of the world. We can interact world over with the help of English language.

The main focus of teaching language is to interact with others orally or in written form. The objectives of teaching English as first language are of four types.

(a) Skill objectives
(b) Cognitive objectives
(c) Attitudinal objectives
(d) Creative objectives

The specific objectives of these areas have been as follows:

(a) The Skill Objectives

A language is known as skill of reading, writing, speaking and listening.

1. The skill of speaking or pronuncing words correctly to express his ideas and feelings to others.

2. The skill of writing or expressing his views and experiences to others.
3. The skill of reading the literature and other subjects to grasp and understand them.
4. To develop the ability of sequence and ratio of pronuncing the words.
5. The skill of listening ideas, views to others, and also to understand them correctly.

The major objective of teaching language is to develop the communicative competency among the students.

(b) The Cognitive Objectives

A language is closely related to a literature which is mainly cognitive in nature. Language learning also requires the knowledge of grammar and structure of sentences.

1. To develop the knowledge and application of grammar.
2. To develop the awareness of phonemes or elements of sound and its proper pronunciation.
3. To develop the knowledge and understanding of morphemes or structure of words and sentences.
4. To develop the ability of appreciation and criticism of ideas and theme of poem and prose.
5. To develop the awareness about poems, stories, novels, drama and essays.

(c) Attitudinal Objectives

This type of objectives is related to affective domain:

1. To develop interest and right type attitude towards language and literature.
2. To develop the interest of reading the supplementary books related to the curriculum.
3. To contribute in essay, story and poem in school magazine.
4. To develop interest in the library and reading room.

5. To encourage the students to participate in discussion, debate and cultural programmes.
6. To develop the interest in reading the religious books and other literature.
7. To create interest in reading newspapers and other literary magazines etc.

(d) Creative Objectives :

A language is used for creating new literature.

1. To encourage students for writing essays, stories, poems and novels etc.
2. To develop the interest of self-study.
3. To encourage the students for composing poems and dialogues.
4. To provide the opportunities for developing original thinking and expressing it.
5. To develop the ability of imagination and reasoning related to some ideas and thinking.
6. To encourage the students to develop their own effective style of writing and expressing the ideas, views, feelings and realisations.

General Objectives of Teaching Mother-tongue

The following are the general objectives of teaching English as first language:

1. To develop four skills — reading, writing, speaking and listening correctly.
2. To develop the ability of expressing ideas, views, feelings and experiences with emotions.
3. To develop the ability of verbal interaction.
4. To develop the ability for expressing his ideas in written form.
5. To develop the moral and character of the students.
6. To develop the awareness about the literature and knowledge of other subjects.

7. To develop the ability and skill for preparing new literature.
8. To prepare good citizen by developing their personality.

The objectives of teaching mother-tongue are classified into three levels— primary, secondary and higher secondary levels. The stage objectives of first language teaching have been given in the following paragraphs.

(a) First Language Teaching Objectives at Primary Stage

The following are the main objectives of teaching English as first language at primary stage:

1. To develop the skill of correct pronunciation of vocabulary.
2. To develop the skill of writing words with correct spellings.
3. To develop the skill of reading the passage correctly.
4. To enrich the English vocabulary.
5. To develop the ability for reciting poems orally.
6. To develop the ability for writing dictation correctly by listening the words.
7. To develop the habit of reading and writing by practice.

(b) Objectives of Teaching English at Secondary Stage

The following are the main objectives of english teaching at secondary level:

1. To develop the knowledge and understanding of grammar.
2. To develop the ability for using grammar in his own writing english.
3. To develop the understanding the meaning of english passage.
4. To develop the interest in reading english textbooks.
5. To develop the habit of self-study.
6. To develop the ability for writing essay and meaning of the passage in his own words.
7. To develop the interest and favourable attitude towards english language.

8. To develop the understanding about rules of grammar and their use in writing english.

(c) Objectives of Teaching English at Higher Secondary Stage

The following are the main objectives at this stage:

1. To encourage and motivate students for more studying english language.
2. To encourage for composing poems and writing essay.
3. To develop the ability for grasping the theme of poem or english passage.
4. To encourage the students for writing the meaning or theme of poem or passage in their own words.
5. To develop the ability of appreciation of ideas and criticising the thinking.
6. To develop the creativity of the students related to verbal ability and reasoning or fluency of language.
7. To develop the ability of understanding of other school subjects.
8. To develop the mastery of language for expressing his ideas, feelings and experiences.
9. To develop the ability of evaluation and analysis of language components.
10. To develop the values, moral and character of the students.

III. Teaching Method

Meaning of method

According to Mackey, "A method determines what and how much is taught (selection), the order in which it is taught (gradation), how the meaning and form are conveyed (presentation), and what is done to make the use of the language unconsciously (repetition). Thus, a method deals with four things:

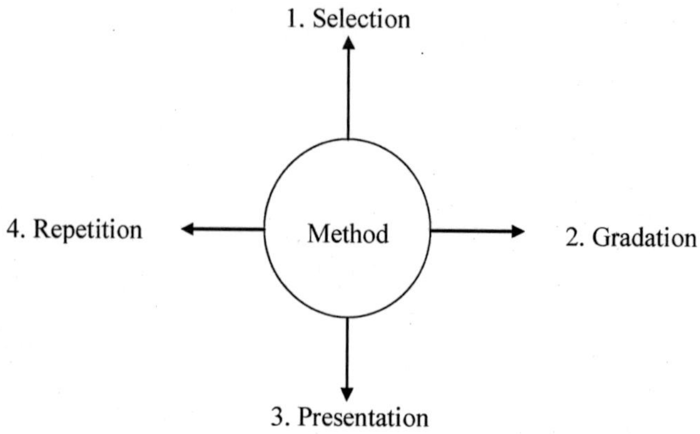

"The Grammar – Translation Method"

Meaning

Translation is to express in one language a serious of ideas presented in another language. It requires a fair knowledge of both the languages. The translation method is the oldest of teaching english in India. In translation method, translation and grammar equally predominated. According to Champion, "under the translation method, the meaning of English words, phrases and sentences are taught by means of word for word translation in the mother tongue".

Principles

According to Thompson and Wyatt this method is based on the following principles:

1. Translation interprets the words and phrases of the foreign language in the best possible way.
2. The foreign phraseology is best assimilated in this process of interpretation.
3. The structures of foreign language are best learnt by comparison and contrast with those in mother tongue.

4. Learning mainly involves the mastery of grammatical rules and memorisation of long lists of literary vocabulary.

Advantages

1. Its approach is direct and simple.
2. The vocabulary is rapidly expanded.
3. The pupils learn the accurate meanings of words and thus this method ensures accuracy.
4. It makes use of the child's knowledge of his mothertongue.
5. Testing of comprehension also becomes easy.

Disadvantages

1. There is little emphasis laid on the activities of listening or speaking.
2. The natural order of learning a language is listening, speaking, reading and writing. As the translation method starts with reading, it is unnatural method.
3. It makes no provision for practice and application of the material presented.
4. It stops with the presentation of lists of words and grammatical rules.
5. Literary translation proves meaningless.
6. Learning a language by rules of grammar is not sound and it leads to uninteresting ritual.

The Direct Method

Meaning

Direct method is also known as the oral or natural method. It is based on the active involvement of the learner in speaking and listening to the foreign language in realistic everyday situations.

According to Webster's New International Dictionary, "Direct method is the method of teaching a foreign language, especially a modern language, through conversation, discussion and reading in the language itself, without translation and without the study of formal grammar".

Main Features of Direct Method

1. Direct contact between word and idea.
2. Inhibition of the mother-tongue.
3. English realign.
4. Prominence of oral work.
5. The sentence as unit.
6. Inductive teaching of grammar.
7. Teaching vocabulary in the context.

Advantages

1. This method teaches language in the same way in which the child learns his mother-tongue.
2. Pupils who are taught through this method converse in english with great ease.
3. Language is taught through demonstration and so this method makes use of audio-visual aids.
4. The gap between pupils active and passive knowledge is narrow.
5. The method is psychologically and linguistically sound.
6. Pupils learn proper spoken english.

Disadvantages

1. It is not an easy method to use in school.
2. It gives too much importance for speaking. But sufficient attention is not paid to reading and writing.
3. Grammar is much neglected.
4. It is a costly method.
5. The speech standard set is too high for a foreigner.
6. Limitations of time are a handicap for a total success of the method.

Dr West's Method

Meaning

The method of teaching proposed by Dr West is known as the

"New method" or "Dr West's method".

Dr West proposed this method mainly to remove some of the limitations of Direct method.

Reasons

Dr West promoted this method for the following reasons:

1. English promotes internationalism and brotherhood.
2. It is a medium of communication among the people of different parts of the world.
3. No Indian language is rich in the field of science and technology.
4. English broadens one's mental faculties and abilities.

Emphasis on Reading Ability

In this method, Dr West emphasised reading abilities. According to him, among the four skills involved in language learning, listening, speaking, reading and writing, the skill of reading is more important since it is a passive skill. Here, Dr West means that passive skill is like the foundation of active work. By reading pupils can develop a taste for English literature and to acquire speaking ability.

Emphasis on Silent Reading

Dr West considered that much stress should be laid on silent reading. Therefore, much time should be given for this. This should not be introduced directly.

Advantages

1. This method initiates pupils for self-activity and develop reading, we can develop comprehensive speaking and writing abilities.
2. It enhances vocabulary of students and it is economical.
3. Pupils do not feel overload of grammatical rules.

Disadvantages

1. It ignores understanding, speaking and writing. Besides, it is impossible to separate reading from understanding, writing and speaking.

2. Without acquiring speech ability pupils cannot have good reading.
3. In practical, life, reading alone is not adequate.

Group method

Language cannot exist in isolation or solitude. Billows say, "Language is a social affair. It is the most important binding element in society". Any language that is learnt must be learnt in social relevance. Language learning becomes effective when the pupils learn in a group. English teachers suffer from the problems of large classes. That is why we need special techniques to handle large classes. Group method is one such technique and here the class will be divided into groups for the purpose of carrying out some definite work.

Individual attention cannot be given in a normal class. The teacher has to reduce the strength of the class by dividing them into groups. As English is a skill subject the skills can be developed only through proper practice. Group method can be used in all aspects of English teaching. The teaher has to split the class into units or groups. Because of this, the whole group gets an opportunity to speak in the class. According to Ryburn, "the group method simply means the dividing of the class into groups for the purpose of carrying out some definite work or scheme or work game. For some purposes, the groups may be large, perhaps only two groups in the class. For other purposes, they may be small with only two pupils in a group".

When we give practice to the whole class, it is called Choral Practice. When we give practice to the groups one after another is called Group Practice. In group practice, the teacher can detect the mistakes committed by the individuals. Grouping may be homogeneous or heterogeneous. Pupils having the same level of achievement, ability, interest and intelligence are grouped into one, and are called homogeneous grouping. Pupils having different level of achievement, ability, interest and intelligence are grouped into one and are called heterogeneous. Each group has all the three levels of achievers – high, mediocre and low in the same number.

After dividing the class into homogeneous or heterogeneous groups, the teacher gives instructions and suggests the activities to be completed in groups. As the groups work individually, the teacher goes round the class, supervises the groups and helps the groups. The teacher should not rest while the pupils work. The teacher does corrections, gives suggestions and makes changes as he looks into the work of the individual. The teacher's work becomes easy as she deals with a small number of pupils at a time. Drills, language games, competitions, projects, dramatics and compositions can be carried out in group method. For reading, writing and spelling also this method is useful and effective.

Group work in reading

Normally, after a model reading by the teacher, the teacher will make the pupils to read. When one student reads aloud the remaining students will be passive. Instead of this, the teacher should read the first sentence and the first group should read after him. If a group makes a mistake the opposing group should put the mistake right.

Group work in using the substitution table

Different groups can be made to read sentences from the substitution table one after another.

Group work in transformation of sentences

For conversions like direct to indirect, active to passive etc., one pupil in a group may be asked to convert the sentence. If his answer is correct, the other pupils in the group may be asked to repeat.

Group work in composition

If the teacher wants to make the students to write an essay, the teacher can divide the class according to sub-headings. Each group will collect information about one sub-heading. When the students have collected the necessary information, they write it down. Then they read it out in the class and make corrections. Finally, the whole class is asked to write essay.

Advantages

- Pupils learn the language in a social setting.
- Weak students get better attention from the teacher.
- Co-operative, healthy competition and leadership qualities are developed.
- Language works like games, competitions and projects can be

undertaken. Each group can be compared by their performance.

- High achievers in each group can help the low achievers in learning.
- All the four skills can be developed.

Disadvantages

- Enthusiastic pupils may dominate while the lazy pupils evade the work.
- While giving oral work the class becomes noisy.
- Close and careful supervision by the teacher is not always possible.

Assignment Method

Assignment method is an effective method that could be used in the classroom instruction. Assignment system has originated from the Dalton Plan. When a work is assigned in amount and time that is called an assignment. It is the method, which lays down a fixed amount of work to be done by a student in a reasonable length of time. A bright student will do it at his earliest and take up other work and the weak one will delay it.

The assignment system caters to the individual differences among the pupils. Some students will be good in one subject or weak in another. There may be brilliant or dull and too good or bad. The class approach cannot help them adequately. The teacher of English should give individual attention to all the students in teaching text, grammar and written work. The teacher should give opportunities to students to read, to write and to do exercises at their own pace and by their own voluntary effort and ability.

In the assignment system, the pupils work under the instructions, help and guidance from the teacher. The pupils are kept active.

Procedure

The teacher prepares the assignment carefully to cover the entire programme. Detailed instructions regarding the study must be given. The teacher should have in mind the previous experience of the pupils, their standard of attainment, the objectives, availability of time, and the mastery level achieved. When the teacher introduces the assignment, recalling the previous experience of the student is necessary. The teacher will then explain and clear the difficulties and outlines the materials to be used. The teacher will allot a time to complete the assignment work. As the pupils do the work in the class the teacher goes round and helps them. After the pupils finish the work the teacher corrects them. When there is some general difficulty the teacher calls the whole class and clarifies the general doubts and difficulties.

Assignments are of two types. They are the school assignment and home assignment. For the school assignment, instructions must be given and the teacher should allot time duration. For home assignments, information on different books must be given. Students must refer to various books and time limit should be given to submit the assignment.

Advantages

- This method gives the pupils, a satisfaction of achievement.
- It develops self-reliance in students.
- The individuals work at their own speed.
- This method keeps the pupils active and not mere receptive listeners.
- It is helpful in the development of advanced reading and writing skills such as note taking, summary writing, paraphrasing, composition writing, organising and illustrating the facts and ideas.

Disadvantages

- Since classes are overcrowded the teacher cannot give individual attention to the pupils.
- It is successful only in the hands of expert teachers.
- A lot of preparation on the part of the teacher is necessary.
- This method is time consuming.
- As systematic teaching is not possible teacher – pupil interaction is absent.
- This method is helpful in developing reading and writing skills alone.

- To give assignments in developing listening and speaking skill we need the help of a language laboratory, which is out of reach for most of the schools.

The Text Book Method

This method is popularly known as Dr West's New Method of Teaching English. It came as a reaction against the direct method. Dr West was of the opinion that reading is the most important aim of language teaching. Due emphasis should be laid on reading aloud and silent reading. At the earliest, the child should be enabled to read with ease and pleasure. His firm belief is that learning to read is by far the shortest road to learning to speak and write it. Dr West is of the opinion that the Indian students get less chances of expressing their ideas through English. They need knowledge of English to collect information from English books. So, they should be given training in reading.

When a child makes progress in reading, he acquires speed and facility. He also acquires a feeling of the language and a passive familiarity with the form of the language.

The main features of Dr West's method are:

- Reading is to be used to fix phraseology.
- Vocabulary should be drilled.
- Vocabulary should secure an active response from the learner.
- Written work should be correlated with oral work.

Advantages

- It helps in developing the reading abilities of the students.
- This method suggests a definite procedure to the learners, which they can follow easily. Thus, it makes the task easy and economical.
- Interpretation ability of the learners is also enhanced.

Disadvantages

- It completely neglects oral work, which is generally considered the foundation for language learning.

- Active skills required for language learning are not given any importance. There is over emphasis on passive skills.
- Grammar and composition works are also neglected in this method.
- Too much time spent on reading naturally causes dullness in the class.
- The method remains incomplete because here the emphasis is only on one skill, i.e. reading with, understanding and not on other skills, i.e., listening, speaking and writing.

Thus, we find that Dr West's method has its advantages and disadvantages. In case English becomes a library language for majority of students in India, it would prove to be very effective provided some practice in oral work is also given at the initial stage.

Playway Method

There should be some activity in teaching English that will bring enjoyment to the students. The teacher is expected to be active, patient, calm and hard working. Learners should be attracted to it. The teachers should have creative minds and must spend good deal of time in planning and preparation for the class.

There should be activity both on the part of the students and the teachers. The idea of play-way in education was expounded and developed by Caldwell Cook in the late 19th century. Children learnt best when they are motivated. The principle of play way in education has been successfully used in Kindergarten and Montessori schools.

English through play-way

- Drills of different types should be used in the classroom. There should be activity on the part of the teachers and students. Drill is a device for fixing the subject matter in the minds of the pupils. There will be clear and thorough understanding of the subject matter. Drills can be given in chorus, in group and then individually.
- Situations should be created and then anything should be taught to the students. Real life can be brought closer to each other.
- Debates, poem recitation contests may be held in the academic

session. A student with distinction must be given due recognition. Conducting such functions should be a common feature in the educational institutions.

- Few interesting games may be used for teaching English in the classrooms.
- When work is given in play children automatically get into learning.

Importance of activity and play-way methods

Modern schools are activity schools, which emphasise the creative aspect of experience. Activities give reality to learning and effective teaching uses all available sources. The child builds self-confidence and develops understanding through work and play in the group. The teacher should furnish rich and purposeful learning experiences for children. The teachers should learn how to develop happy relationships with pupils both at work and play.

Types of activities

Activities will vary according to the age-group of pupils, in the kindergarten stage activities like singing, dramatising, listening, observing, collecting, talking, experimenting and constructing are useful. Activities grow as the child grows.

1. Exploratory – knowledge getting,
2. Constructive – experience getting, and
3. Expressional – presentation.

These are the different types of activities. In modern education, creative activities occupy a prominent place. Education for children should be rich enough to meet all needs in a way that will contribute to society.

Play is said to be the language of the child. Play affords a safer release of physical and mental energy and relieves emotional tension. "Play" in the words of Froebel, "is the highest phase of child development. Play is the purest, most spiritual activity of man at this stage, and at the same time, typical of human life as a whole – of the inner-hidden natural life in man and all things. It gives, therefore, joy, freedom, contentment, inner and outer rest, and peace with the world. It holds the source of all that is good.

The Playway in Education

Play is the natural need of the child and Caldwell Cook is the first person, who advocated "way to play" for educating the child. Caldwell Cook believed that proficiency and learning come not from reading and listening but from actions and from experience. He regarded play as a means of training individuals and a wonderful technique of making school education interesting.

Use of Playway Method in English Classroom

- It provides activity-centered teaching. The learners feel interested and they are able to learn things, which are retained in the minds for a long time.
- It provides entertainment to the students. They learn things and at the same time they are able to amuse themselves.
- A number of instincts of the children like self-assertion, self-submission, laughing, etc., are satisfied.
- The subject matter taught is brought nearer to reality and linked with the real life of the child.
- It is the most active way of learning and acquiring some knowledge.
- By this method, the children work whole-heartedly. They are also able to acquire many social and moral values.
- The learners develop fellow-enthusiasm and energy. The play may makes learning real and practical. It has rendered drill work lively instead of being monotonous. Through playway the child learns the best and retains the best. Play is instinctive in its appeal during childhood. It is one of the most effective forces in stimulating effort and developing useful habits.

Language Games

Drills of different types should be used.

They include:

- Substitution drill,

- Repetition drill,
- Conversion drill, and
- Completion drill.

In reception drill, pupils observe the teacher and they repeat by imitating him in every way. This can be used to teach sounds in English. In conversion drill, the learners of a language are asked to convert a sentence into another. This drill is useful to teach transformation of sentence – present to past, assertive to interrogative, active to passive, etc. In completion drill, the teacher gives some model sentences and then provides them with incomplete sentences. The pupils are required to complete them.

Reading Games

The class can be divided into two groups: A and B. The groups should be equally matched as far as possible. The first boy from a should read the sentence from the flash card given to him. If he reads correctly, he scores a mark and the next turn goes to a boy from group 'B'. If a boy makes a mistake, one is the opposite group gets a chance. The teacher is the umpire and all the cases of doubts are referred to him.

Matching games may also be organised. Short sentences or words are written on the flash cards and the pupils should match the sentences and words with corresponding picture cards. Playing with order cards is also a type of language game useful for reading exercises. Simple orders are written on the cards and flashed before the class. The pupils have to read the order and obey.

The conversion game is another type where the class is divided into two groups with conversion cards having a question, and its answer written on it. Each pupil should ask the question written on his card. The pupil from the other group has to give the answer. Marks are given for each correct answer. Word building games are useful in building up the vocabulary.

- A number of letters are written on the black board. The pupils are then asked to write down as many words as possible using the letters given.
- Pupil may be asked to substitute one word for a group of words.

Spelling Bee

The whole class can prepare a difficult passage from which the teacher makes a list of words and fires them at members of each team in turn.

Team Quiz

Each member can ask his *vis-à-vis* in the team any question that begins with Where? What? In turn, he has to answer such question.

The success of the games and the game-like activities that a teacher plans depend on the class organisation.

The Substitution Method

Meaning

The three principal ways of constructing a sentence are:

(i) Grammatical construction, (ii) Conversion and (iii) Ergonic substitution. This method employs ergonic substitution.

Substitution can be defined as a process by which a model sentence may be multiplied infinitely by substitution for any of its words.

We use ergonic substitution in teaching English. This method makes learning easy as well as effective.

For example My book is red.

Procedure

1. The teacher prepared a model sentence based on the previous knowledge of the students.
2. The teacher speaks the model sentences and does not write on the blackboard.
3. The sentence is repeated and then explained by writing on the chalkboard.
4. The pupils are asked to repeat the sentences after the teacher's presentation.
5. Pupils copy the sentence into their notebooks.

Types of substitution drills

The boy The man	killed	a mouse A tiger
The hunter	caught	two birds
An old man	shot	a snake

In the above table, any item in the column can be made use of with every item in the other column to make grammatically correct sentence. The learner can make correct sentences by choosing the item for any column. Such a table is called a Fool proof Table.

How many	boys		in the classroom?
	girls		in the field?
How many		are there	
	books		in the bag?
	marbles		on the table

In this the learner should select the nouns, and the adverbial to avoid non-sensible sentences. Such tables are called Non fool proof tables.

Advantages

1. This method develops all the four skills.
2. It gives practice to the pupil and eliminates the wrong habits developed by the pupils.
3. Different structures are taught interestingly.
4. A large number of sentences are mastered within a short period.

5. This method is logical as it takes the sentence as the unit.
6. Grammar is taught inductively.
7. Pupils develop analytical knowledge.
8. Students are kept active.

Disadvantages

1. All the sentence patterns cannot be taught in this method.
2. Pupils learn isolated sentences and hence there is no sequence.
3. Grammatical sentences and vocabulary alone can be taught using this method.
4. It is skill-oriented but not exam-oriented.

IV. The Structural Approach

The direct method and other methods highlight the importance of exposing the learner to the target language. They were experimental in nature and slowly "they began to fade into forms which gave importance to listening and speaking". Linguists agree that a language should be studied as a living body of communication rather than as a body of rules governing speech and writing. In modern education too much importance are sounds, words and structures. In using these tools, certain skills are to be developed. They are ability to understand the spoken language ability to speak the language, ability to read and to write the language.

In order to learn the language, and various skills of the language, the learner should know its structures. An approach tells us what to teach. 'The structural approach' was introduced in our country in 1950's. Menon and Patel point out "The structural approach is based on the belief that the learning of a foreign language mastery of structure is more important than the acquisition of vocabulary". Structures provide the essential framework of the language. Structures that are provided to the students form the basis of the entire learning procedure.

While teaching English through structural approach certain principles have to be kept in mind. This approach aimed at developing the listening and speaking skill which would form the foundation to develop the skills of reading and writing. The audio-lingual method is called the structural approach in Britain. It is also called the aural-oral method.

Principles on which the method is based

- Language is speech, not writing;
- Language is a set of habits;
- Teach the language, not about the language;
- A language is what its native speaker says – not what someone thinks, and
- Languages are different.

Language is speech not writing

Here, the emphasis is on correct intonation. Listening and speaking should be taught before reading and writing. The mastery of oral skills should precede reading and writing which will act as reinforces.

Language is a set of habits

This implies that language has to be given in terms of language patterns.

Teach the language not about the language.

Active practice becomes more meaningful and effective.

- The three basic principles of sentence construction in English are word order.
- Use of structural words, and
- Inflexions.

Word order

In English words are to be arranged in a fixed word order to give meaningful sentences. The arrangement and position of words kept in order make the sentence pattern.

For example, The elephant killed the man,

The man killed the elephant.

The change in the order of words show change in meaning.

Use of structural words

English depends more on their usage in sentence construction. Words such as prepositions, articles, pronouns, relative pronouns, auxiliaries or helping verbs, conjunctions, structural adjectives and structural adverbs play a significant role in deciding the meaning of a sentence. Such words are called structural words.

For example,

Does she dances?

Will she dance?

Should she dance?

Could she dance?

These sentences are different because of the use of structural words like does, will, should and could.

In the case of phrases, we find they are different because of the use of structural words.

For example,

Over the table, under the table, on the table, and from the table.

Here, the structural words are very simple and they have no meaning of their own.

Inflexions

English is noted for its inflexions. Inflexions refer to the changes or differences in the form of words to show the different parts or roles that take in a sentence. Small differences in the form of words and sentences. The element of change in spelling and pronunciation is called inflexions.

For example,

Girl	Girls
Woman	Women

According to Jesperson structures are of two types:

(a) Conventional,

(b) Sentence pattern.

The conventional structures are expressions accepted in common usage like greetings and leave taking (hair, hello, bye, good day). The second type of structure comprises sentence patterns which may vary in words but not in form.

A man went to temple,

A girl went to temple, and

A teacher went to temple.

F.G. French has given the basic structural pattern for the simple sentence in English.

1. Two parts pattern – S + V

   Lion roars

2. Three parts pattern – S + V + O

   I learn grammar

3. Four parts pattern – S + V + P + O

   She gave him a book

4. Patterns with "there"

   There are the tables

5. Questions beginning with a verb

   Did you go there?

6. Questions beginning with an asking word

   Who are you? What did he do?

7. Commands or requests

   Open the windows

   Shut the door

Principles for the Selection of Structures

The basic structures are so carefully selected, graded and systematically planned that every structure is followed by one based on the previous one. The selection and grading involve an assessment of the ability of the average learner, the time given to the teaching of the subject, the capacity of the teachers, and the availability of the material. In selecting structures, the following principles are to be followed.

Usefulness

The usefulness of a structure is determined on the frequency of its occurrence both in spoken and written language. Usefulness depends upon frequency in use and helpfulness in further building of the language.

Simplicity

The simplicity of structure depends upon its form and meaning. Simple structures are to be taught earlier. Difficult ones have to be taken up later.

Productivity

Productivity means a number of structures can be produced one after another. No item should be taught in isolation. The various items should be linked with one another.

Teachability

If a structure is more easily demonstrated in a realistic situation, it can be more teachable than the other. The structures which are easy from teaching point of view should be given preference.

Grading the structures

Grading is to put the teaching material in a suitable order. The teaching of structures should be spread throughout the course. Structures should be taught along with the content words. While grading the material the chronological age of the children has to be kept in mind.

Teaching of Structures

1. Oral teaching : Aural-Oral method is the most suitable for teaching the structures. The teacher may be given oral drill to the class in chorus, groups and then to individuals. C.C. Fries says, “The speech is the language. The written record is a secondary representation of the language. To master a language is not necessary to read it, but it is extremely doubtful whether one can really read the language without mastering it orally”.

2. Situational teaching : Anything taught or learnt in a situation is more meaningful. It makes teaching or learning more realistic. The situation makes the structure easily understandable. Situation should be appropriate to the structure in hand. Otherwise, it will lead to confusion.

Classroom techniques - teaching structures

The term structure refers to a sequence of linguistic units that are in a certain relationship to one another. For example, 'one of the structures of a noun phrase'—a group of words with a noun or pronoun as the main part—a non-phrase may consist of only one word (as in George arrived yesterday) or it may be a complex one as in:

The students who enrolled late, and who have not yet filled in their cards must do so by Friday, may be 'article + adjective + noun' as in a structure like the friendly ape.

Let us now look at fragments of dialogues.

A: Excuse me; can you come with me to the city?

B: I'm afraid I can't.

A: Excuse me; do you know what time the bus leaves?

B: I'm afraid I don't.

A: Is there anything I can do about it?

B: I'm afraid there is not.

By now you will have identified the structural pattern in the above, fragments. Yes, 'I'm afraid...+ n't.

In teaching a structure, the first step is to make the learners recognise the pattern.

The following are some of the techniques that you can use in presenting new structures.

1. Make your (as mentioned earlier) learner recognise the pattern by giving 'model sentences'. These are sentences for oral practice which show the connection between a point that your pupils already know, and the new one that you are teaching them. If these sentences only contain vocabulary, that your students already know, you can write them straight up on the board. For example, 'some' is already known to them, and you are introducing 'any' in negative sentences.

Model sentences

He hasn't any beacon. The news agents' get some newspapers. He hasn't any stamps. In many ways, however, it is better to use model sentences in dialogue form, which make the sentences a natural exchange.

'I'd like some mutton, please'. 'I'm sorry, we haven't any mutton'.

'I'd like some lamb, please'. 'I'm sorry. We haven't got any lamb.'

You could follow on in the various things that other shopkeepers have and haven't got. This would lead naturally into drills and dialogues.

Dialogues: We can introduce structures with straight forward dialogues where the meaning of a new structure is clear, and where it is used appropriately, for example, suppose you are introducing don't with main verbs.

A: Excuse me. Where's K.R. Market?

B: Where? I don't understand?

A: K.R. Market

B: Oh - K.R. Market. I don't know.

A: You don't know;

B: No. I don't live here. I'm from Madras. You can also get such dialogues acted out.

Situation: Presentation is always clearer and more meaningful, if it is part of an actual situation or brief story. For example, let's assume that one of us is planning a trip to some place, or assume you are going to visit Bombay. What are you going to do before hand? You may say this.

'I'm going to pack clothes, a tooth brush etc., say goodbye to my family take a bus to the airport or railway station.' This kind of presentation would lead to what students would do as individuals.

Demonstration: By bringing things into the classroom, we can present structures. Prepositions can be effectively introduced using this technique. An essential part of demonstration involves bringing things into the classroom; 'mime' can be used here. Description or narrative: You can produce a story or description with a structure and vocabulary that the students already know, but introduce a new structure that is unfamiliar. Grammatical statements or using good rules can help students: Teachers have believed that stating rules confused students, so they have simply presented a larger group of examples and their students have practiced them. The sequence (rules - examples and practise) has been often discussed, as have the rules themselves. An understanding of the nature of language rules helps teachers and students. A few teachers still believe in prescriptive rules—rules which tell us what 'should' and 'should not' be possible in the language. This is a mistake—all linguists believe rules should be descriptive—they should say how the language is used not how it would be used.

Controlled practice in saying useful and correct sentence patterns in combination with appropriate vocabulary. These patterns are known as oral drills. They can be inflexible, students often seem to master a structure by drilling, but are then incapable of using it in other contexts. Drills therefore should be:

(i) Realistic—don't get students to practise sentences they would never actually say in real life.

(ii) Meaningful—practice should take place within a context.

(iii) Said with appropriate expressions—e.g., surprise, impatience, enthusiasm, indifference, etc.

(iv) Used for only a minute or two.

(v) Use of signs and pictures and sound prompts gives briskness and interest to the practice.

(vi) Used as a first stage, quickly leading the way to other kinds of practice.

Types of drills

1. Listening and repetition drill.
2. Simple substitution drill—The basic sentence pattern the students are then required to substitute different items in a given place in the sentence and say the sentence with that structure.

e.g., let's take for example, the practise of did you see that aeroplane?

Prompt: aeroplane did you see that car?

car, bus

boy, girl

Variable substitution drill

Give the model sentence, then the prompt, they are to substitute, which requires them to think and change something in the rest of the sentence.

3. Diagrams. Diagrams can be used for presenting certain structures. For example, preposition.

4. Progressive substitution drill: Give the model sentence. Then give prompts that have to be substituted in different parts of the sentence, and which may require alteration of other words. As this drill is more complicated, it is not so useful for initial practice but is ideal for the quick revision of different points, and really makes the students think.

For example, If John argues, I'll be angry.

Prompt: Mary-students

Argues, If Mary argues, I'll be angry.

They,....................................

Furious ....

David ....

Disagree..............................

The student has to work out where the prompt goes in the sentence. If there are two alternatives, he can choose between them.

Situationalised drill: Giving an example using the set phrase or structural item you wish to practise giving prompts and going on to paired practise.

For example, the phrase that's bad lucks.

I've failed my exam. That is bad luck. I've broken my leg.

That is bad luck.

The first speaker might express courageous resignation while the second expresses genuine concern.

Substitution tables: These are written on the board. The student chooses what he wants to say. Be careful when constructing tables as it is very easy to produce strange combinations. Vocabulary should already be familiar and attention has to be paid on stress. Tables are useful for simultaneous revision, or practising idiomatic phrases. Substitution tables bridge speaking and reading. Once your students are familiar with a structure or with vocabulary orally they can consolidate spelling and pronunciation through reading appropriate sentences aloud. Substitution tables can be used for the formation of large members of correct sentences, if substitution tables are over used the novelty will soon wear off, so it is as well to vary the way we use them in class. The following are just a few of the ways in which we can make substitution tables more challenging for our students.

1. One' column'of the table can be missed out.
2. Certain words can be missed out.
3. Picture prompts can replace some of the words.
4. Writing from the tables can be turned into a game by giving a certain time limit and seeing who can make the most sentences.
5. Interest can be increased by increasing student participation.
6. The teacher can erase sections of the table and get the students to make different but correct replacements.
7. The teacher can get the students to read the table and then he can gradually erase parts of it. The teacher can erase only a small part of the table, half or nearly all of it, depending on the ability of the students.

Note that in presenting a structure much more time should be spent on practice than on presentation. Practice can take many different forms and basically when planning his work, the teacher needs to take into consideration the following stages.

Presentation: The presentation stage has a few steps as given below:

(i) Controlled practice,

(ii) Free practice (production),

(iii) Checking that the structure has been learnt.

(iv) Further practice—this could take the form of practice in further situations or in combination with a new structure dealt with later, consolidation, revision or if necessary remedial work.

Controlled practice— this is the stage at which learners are given intensive practice in the new structure, but their production of the language is very carefully guided, and controlled by the teacher, so that correct form and meaning are consolidated and the possibility of error is reduced to a minimum.

This traditional way takes the form of some kind of drill. Drills can be (a) clause combination drill (b) mini-dialogue drill (c) question drill (d) expansion drill (e) progressive substitution drill (f) simple substitution drill (g) variable substitution drill, and (h) situational drill.

From controlled practice, we have to aim at free practice. A communicative drill fits into this.

Let us look at the following activity, and say how the information gap is created.

Group A

Ask your partner the times of trains to five of these places. Write down what he tells you.

Bombay........ Dharmavaram.

Calcutta........ New Delhi.......

Manias......... Bangalore........

Trivandrum....

Group B

Give your partner the information he asks for.

Bombay 9.00-21.00

Madras 6.30; 7.45; 13.15; 21.45

Calcutta -13.15; 22.45

Trivandrum - 8.45; 19.25

New Delhi -19.30; 20.30

This exercise creates an information gap so that there can be a more realistic question, and answer drill as information is actually passed from A to B (or *vice-versa)*.

The exercise is arranged in such a way that the person spending does not even know which question is next. "But this is not in itself enough to make Group A, Listen and Process. It is necessary but not a sufficient condition. If the student is not asked to write anything down, 'he would have no reason to listen. He is not being asked to do anything with the information he has been given; hence he has no motivation for listening and processing'. It is the instruction,' write down what he tells you, that makes the exercise truly communicative. These words make the exercise conform to a principle important in communicative language teaching—the principle of getting the student to utilise in some way information given in the course of an exercise."

This process is adaptable to structure drills. Attempt to produce such communicative drills while teaching structures.

Advantages

1. The vocabulary items and structures are carefully selected and graded and so learning becomes easier.
2. As language is speech and not writing much importance is given to speech.
3. Teaching items are taught in appropriate and meaningful situations.
4. The pupils cultivate the habit of speaking the language.
5. Students are active as they are given opportunities to speak out and practice the structures.

Limitations

1. Reading, writing and vocabulary expansion are neglected in this approach.
2. Structural approach emphasises drill work. But, this drill work will become a mechanical activity.
3. As suitable teachers are not available this approach suffers in the hands of inexperienced teachers. Though, the textbooks are written according to the structural approach, the teachers do not know how to present or drill the structures.

V. The Situational Approach

Language is always used in reference to a particular context or situation. Language relies much on situations. C.C. Fries says,

"The only true and correct meanings of words are the situations in which they are used. A word consists of a sound or a combination of sounds, that has become conventionalised in a culture or a linguistic community, that is used in certain situations and that stimulates certain responses in the hearer belonging to the same community".

A word or structure becomes meaningful only when it is used in appropriate situation. To comprehend the meaning, the learner must grasp the situation. When the language is used spontaneously in meaningful situations he can comprehend it without any conscious effort.

There are four types of situation namely real life situations, classroom situations, imaginary situations and verbal situation.

Situations, which the child can hear, and touch in the classroom, are classroom situations. The objects inside the classroom are used to create situations. Classroom situations are very interesting for young children.

Situations, which the pupils know from his own experience in his daily life, and his family circle, are real life situations. It is the previous personal experience. The teacher makes the students to recall their experiences and thus creates the situation.

Situations, which can be called, to mine through imagination with the help of pictures, maps, charts, plans, dramatisation, and other visual aids are imaginary situations.

Situations, which are brought into the minds of the pupils through the spoken, written or printed words, are verbal situations. Such situations are created mainly through descriptions without the help of A.V. aids. In the higher classes, verbal situations can be used.

Situations can be either real or artificial. Learning becomes effective when we use real situations. Real objects are shown to the students. When real objects cannot be brought to the class, we make use of models, pictures and conversations. This kind of artificial setting is known as contrived situation.

The various situations discussed above can be summarised as below:

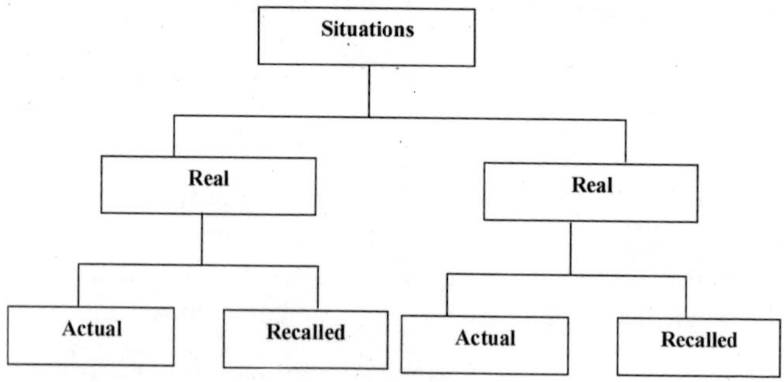

In selecting the situation, the following order of preference should be kept in mind:

- Actual,
- Recalled,
- Visualised, and
- Verbal.

The teacher has to create situations in the classroom as situations stimulate the pupils to express themselves in learning the aspects of a new language. Degrees of comparison and prepositions can be taught using real objects. Though gestures and actions also we can create situations. Gestures and actions are effective in teaching commands, requests, questions and sentence patterns.

By using models, charts and pictures situations can be created. Pictures in the Reader, Wall pictures and albums help the teacher in creating situations. If the teacher is an expert in blackboard drawing, simple matchstick diagrams can be used to create situations.

Merits

- Situational approach serves as a very good motivating tool for the pupils.
- It makes group work effective.
- It makes the language teaching more effective and interesting.

- This approach makes the pupils to get mastery over vocabulary and language items quickly.

Demerits

- The situational approach makes an inexperienced teacher think that each situation is suitable.
- It may be ridiculous to follow in higher classes.
- The teacher may find it difficult to cover the portion in time.

The best kind of language course is psychologically based on the context of situation. From this spring motivation and interest and the development of proper bonds between language and skills in its use. The good organisation of the language course relies on identifying and constructing appropriate contexts or situations.

VI. Communicative Approach

Introduction

'Speech is species specific'

Communicative approach was adopted in the early Eighties. In this approach, 'fluency is the goal, not accuracy'. The teacher is just a co-ordinator of classroom activities. It is a learner-centred approach.

There are three determinants of communication.

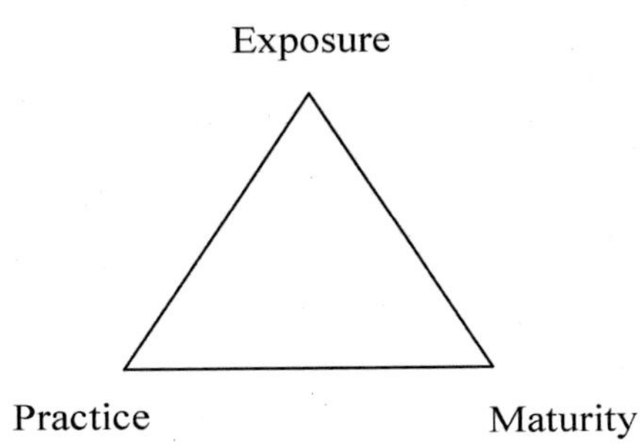

Communication

Communication means exchange of ideas, thoughts, feelings and opinions. Language being the foremost means of communication, it should be taught mainly for communicative purpose. Language is a vehicle for communication, and when we use language for communication we must have knowledge of the linguistic forms of the language.

Approach

Approach deals with assumptions. Within one approach, there can be many methods.

Meaning of communicative approach

- Communicative approach pays attention to functional as well as structural aspects of languages and combines these into a more fully communicative view.
- Communicative approach emphasises that the goal of foreign language teaching is to develop 'communicative ability' among the learners.
- This approach considers language not only in terms of its structures but also in terms of communicative functions that it performs.
- Communicative approach emphasised that it is not enough to teach learner the structures of the foreign language alone. They must use these structures in their communications in real situations.

Importance of communicative approach

- The learner is helped to acquire language forms to their potential functional and social meaning.
- The learner is place in situations and he must use language as an instrument for satisfying communicative needs. The criterion for success in functional effectiveness rather than structural accuracy.
- The learner can be helped to use language as an instrument for social interaction. Here, the communicative effectiveness and the social acceptability of the language used are emphasised.

Purpose of communicative activities

Communicative ability can be achieved through communicative activities in the class. Communication activities are learner-directed activities. They can:

- Provide structural whole task practice,
- Improve motivation,
- Allow natural learning, and
- Create a context which supports learning.

Type of communicative activities

There are two main categories of communicative activities.

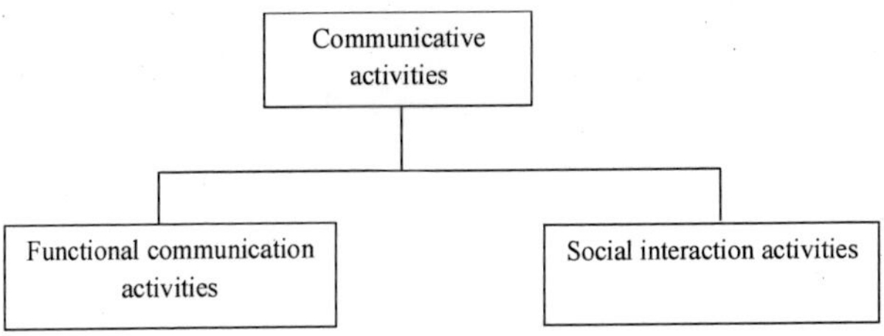

1. Functional Communication Activities

The teacher creates a situation in which learners must solve a problem, with whatever language they have at their disposal. It may not even matter whether the language they use is grammatically incorrect. The main purpose of his activity is that learners should use the language they know.

For example, a small talk on a particular topic for just three minutes is an activity for functional communication. Success is measured primarily according to whether they cope with the communicative demands of the immediate situation.

2. Social Interaction Activities

Here, the learner chooses the language which is not only functionally effective, but is also appropriate to the social situations he is in.

Learners pay greater attention to the social context in which the interaction takes place.

Simulation and role playing are important techniques for creating a wider variety of social situations.

Communicative competence

Communicative competence is an ability not only to apply the grammatical rules of a language in order to form grammatically correct sentences, but also to know when and where to use the sentences.

It includes,

- Knowledge of the grammar and vocabulary of the language.
- Knowing how to use and respond to different types of speech acts such as requests, thanks, etc.
- Knowing how to use the language appropriately.

Thus, communicative competence includes

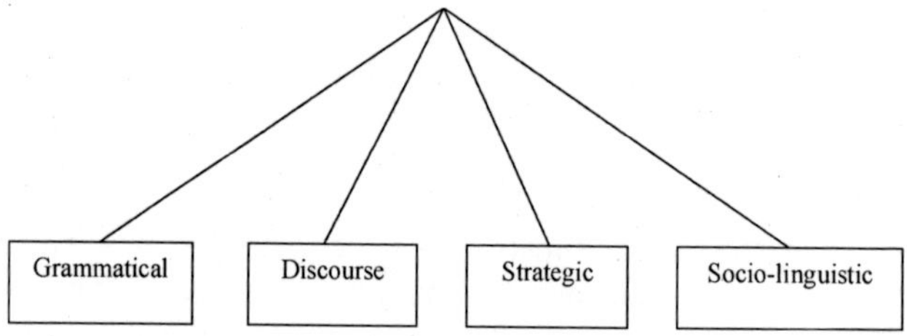

Grammatical competence

It is known as 'linguistic competence'. It is the communication knowledge of grammar and vocabulary.

Discourse competence

It is the interpretation of individual message elements in terms of,

- The context,
- Relation in which the discourse takes place, and
- The inter-connectedness of these elements.

Strategic competence

It refers to strategies that communicators employ to initiate, terminate, maintain, repair and redirect communication.

Socio-linguistic competence

It refers to an understanding of the social context in which communication takes place.

Teacher's role in communicative approach

The teacher must :

- Stress on oral communication not bothering about systematic grammar rules.
- Create situations in which pupils express their ideas and suggestions.
- Insist on meaning in speech activity more than anything else.
- Develop confidence in pupils that their mistakes are not barriers for communication.
- Mediawares like T.V, video can be used often.
- Give language exercises which will bring out the originality and creativity of pupils ideas.
- Be a perfect model in speech.
- Let the pupil absorb lexis and structure unconsciously.
- Create situations where the pupils speak more and more on their own.
- At the later stage, make pupils describe things and explain functions of certain organs, etc.

During these activities the teacher acts as an advisor, answering student's questions and monitoring their performance.

Procedures in communicative language teaching

The teacher presents a brief dialogue preceded by a motivation and discussion of the function and situation – people, setting, roles, topic and the informality and formality of the language.

The teacher allows oral practice of each utterance of the dialogue either in chorus or individually. The oral practice is preceded by the teacher's model.

The teacher sets questions based on the dialogue practiced and elicits answers.

The teacher sets questions based on the student's personal experiences. He takes care that the experience centres on the dialogue theme.

Teacher reads one of the basic communicative expressions in the dialogue.

Teacher gives a few more example of the function, using pictures, real objects or dramatisation to clarify the meaning of the function.

Helps learners to discover rules underlying the functional expression or structure.

Teacher gives activities that would encourage and recognise the function.

Teacher makes the students to copy the dialogue, if they are not in the text.

Advantages

- Through this approach, the very aim of language learning is realised.
- This approach ensures active participation of the students.
- Students are able to manipulate the structures of languages correctly.
- The teacher is active and innovative, as he has to set the stage.

Disadvantages

- This approach envisages a great responsibility on the part of the teacher.
- This approach requires devoted teachers.

- All the areas of communicative competence cannot be tested and all the functions of English cannot be taught.
- It needs a lot of flexibility on the part of the syllabus as the ability of the learners varies according to their social environment and status.
- This approach is time-consuming, and it requires the co-operation of the learner.

Importance of communicative approach

- The learner is helped to acquire language forms to their potential functional and social meaning.
- The learner is place in situations, and he must use language as an instrument to satisfying communicative needs.
- The learner can be helped to use language as an instrument for social interaction, to example through role-playing activities. Here, the communicative effectiveness, and the social acceptability of the language used are emphasised.

Purpose of communicative activities

Communicative ability can be achieved through communicative activities in the class. They are:

- Provide structured "whole-task practice".
- Improve motivation,
- Allow natural learning, and
- Create a context which supports learning.

Types of communicative activities

1. Group work : The objective is to help the learners use the new language function in the small group, talk to one another, ask questions, find patterns that will constitute the correct answers, reorganise the answers for the use of different patterns, and the use of communicative expressions that are essential part of conversational English.

2. Pair work : Here, the class will be divided into groups of two as they are reacted in the class. No re-arrangement is necessary, inter-questioning as a technique is the best for pair-work. The greatest advantage of pair-work is that into is a very simple-method, that the whole class is kept active everyone will get involved into it.

3. Role play : The individual in the society is a role-player. Language is employed as a vehicle to give expression to these roles in a variety of ways. In this teaching, these natural roles in society are stimulated in the classroom.

4. Dramatisation : It includes a variety of activities right from simple enactment of piece of conversation upto same form of a skill in which whole short them can be handled. Role play is simple dramatisation which can be complex.

5. Miming : In this, the student will be engaged in the process of imitating some character. The teacher guides the imitation by the student or does the imitation himself which as he same time students are asked to interpret, and say what is being done. It can be easily to be carried out in the classroom context.

6. Reporting observation : This is highly practical activity. The learners can be asked to (a) measure the size of things and rooms and report the measurement in English. So, every reporting is to be reported in English.

7. Inter-questioning : A group-work or pair work can integrate this work. The questions can be written on a piece of paper, and the pupils can look at those and ask the questions. Every time, the question is asked and answer provide which will create good atmosphere.

8. Work on picture : Pictures, sketches, and charts can be employed for very creative use in a communicative language teaching a group or a pair can be asked to produce communicative sentences and expressions from the picture.

9. Work on models : Same as picture, by keeping models, the students are asked to talk about that.

10. Making of guess : Each pupil has to make a guess, and say what the teacher had asked already. Here, the students will develop their vocabulary and the language can be produced. This can be done before whole class or in group.

11. Talking about John : The students are asked to talk few minutes about their friends. This constitutes fine material for communicative language practice.

12. Reporting TV/Video scenes : By seeing the programme in television and videos, the scenes are to be reported in front of the class. Here, there will create a communication skill among the students.

Teacher's role in communicative approach

- Stress on oral communication not bothering about systematic grammar rules.

VII. Teaching of English Prose

Definition of prose

According to Coleridge, "Prose is words in their best order". The nature, aims, and methods of teaching prose are different from those of poetry. Prose appeals to the head. Prose is more sight than sound merely patterns in paper. There is no rhythm in prose. It is for mere information and knowledge.

Characteristics of prose

Prose is words in their best descriptive order. Prose consists of philosophical ideas, social problems, and historical description of events, geographical concepts and economical conditions of the society. Prose is used to develop the cognitive and effective aspects of students.

Prose develops the language skills, reading, and writing, speaking and listening. Prose enriches the vocabulary of the students, and develops the ability of explaining theme and to grasp the ideas of the writer.

General objective of teaching prose

(i) To enable students to understand the passage and grasp its meaning.

(ii) To enable the pupils to read English passage loudly with correct pronunciation, stress, intonation, and articulation of voice.

(iii) To enable them to understand the passage by silent reading.

(iv) To enable them to express ideas of the passage orally and in writing.

(v) To enable them to enjoy reading and writing.

(vi) To enable them to get knowledge contained in the lesson.

(vii) To develop their imaginative powers, and

(viii) To prepare them for world citizenship.

Specific objectives of teaching prose

Specific objectives vary according to the subject matter of the prose lessons. A prose lesson may be descriptive or a story, biography play or an essay. The specific aims of these types of prose lessons are:

(a) Descriptive

- To acquaint pupils with the style of the writer,
- To develop the imaginative powers of students.

(b) Story

- To give knowledge of some facts through the story,
- To teach some lesson through the story,
- To train students character, and
- To develop the students power of imagination.

(c) Essay

- To get students receive knowledge,
- To make them curious about the subject of the essay, and
- To enable them to arrange ideas in a systematic way.

(d) Composition

- To enable the students to write correct English with reasonable speed,
- To develop students imaginations power, and
- To increase the vocabulary of students.

(e) Biography

- To get students acquainted with the lives and deeds of great men.

- To show them the path or character-building,
- To increase their love of aspiration, and
- To follow the teaching of great men of the world.

(f) Play or drama

- To teach student with play-way method,
- Giving them opportunities for self-expression,
- To make them play different roles, and
- To build their character.

Procedure

Introduction

Teacher starts the question by asking some introductory questions in order to test the knowledge of the students. He may attract the students' attention by saving pictures, models, etc. He should aim at arousing the curiosity of the class.

Statement of Aim

The teacher should clearly and concisely explain the aim on the objective of that day and should ask the students to open their books at the appropriate page.

Presentation

This is the main part of the lesson and plan the teacher must present the lesson in an interesting and efficient manner to the students. The lesson may be taught in one or two units. However, if the lesoon is short, it can be taught in any are unit.

Model Reading by Teacher

Teacher reads aloud and selected passage. Paying careful attention to pronunciation, phrases and intonation. The speed of reading should be normal, and is reading should be audible to the entire class.

Pronounciation Drill

Pronounciation drill should precede reading aloud. The words should be selected on the basis of the pronunciation skill of the class. Thus, words which are incorrectly pronounced should be chosen for practice.

Reading aloud by students

The teacher asks some students to read the passage aloud one by one. This helps to correct the students' pronunciation, and to improve the tone, rhythm and fluency of reading.

Exposition of difficult words/structures

Vocabulary, grammar and structures are the most important components of a prose lesson. The teacher selects the new words and phrases from the passage, and explains their meaning clearly. The teacher may use the Direct/Translation/Usage/Similar word method.

VIII. Teaching of Poetry

Introduction

Musical and metrical form of language is poetry. Poetry is a thing of beauty of form, beauty of thought and beauty of emotions. It is intimately limited with life.

"Poetry is made out of life, belong to life, and exist for life".

—- Hudson

Coleridge defines poetry as, "The best words in their best order".

According to S. Subrahmanyam, "Poetry is a thing of beauty: beauty of form, beauty of thought, mood and feelings".

In other words, we may say that poetry is beauty. It is the beauty of language, beauty of thought, mood or feeling. It is the most intimate expression of man's spirit.

Importance of Teaching Poetry

Poetry is regarded as the noble thoughts and noble emotions caught in noble language. Its main importance in the classroom is that it brings the students into contact with the human nature, and also with feelings, and aspirations of great souls. It enriches their emotional life and develops the aesthetic sense among them. Students get pleasure through rhythm and rhyme of poetry. Children are very fond of poetry due to its musical sounds and rhythms. Hence, poetry occupies an important place in school curriculum.

Advantages and Limitations of Teaching Poetry

Advantages

Teachings of poetry to students have following advantages:

(i) It helps in all-round development of pupils, as pointed out by S. Subrahmanyam "the value of teaching poetry in English language course at the secondary school level is immense. It leads to an all-round development of a whole personality of pupils, particularly the emotional, imaginative, intellectual, aesthetic and intuitive sides".

(ii) It enriches the experiences of the pupils.

(iii) It facilitates the natural aptitude for poetry in pupils.

(iv) It enables students to learn speech rhythm through the rhythm of poetry.

(v) It has cathartic value, because it helps in expression and training of emotions. According to Billow, "there seems to be a special value in poetry in a foreign language in opening up the fantasy and giving release to inhibited, and excessively introverted types".

(vi) Poetry always imparts enjoyment and pleasure to students.

(vii) It introduces variety.

(viii) It teaches pattern sentences because of repetition of certain patterns in a poem.

Limitations

In the opinion of some scholars, teaching of poetry is redundant and unnecessary. Following arguments are given against poetry teaching:

(i) English is a foreign language for Indian pupils, so they cannot understand and appreciate the beauty of poetry.

(ii) Poetry does not facilitate the linguistic aim of teaching English.

(iii) In poetry, pupils have to face vague ideas, unusual words and different words order.

(iv) It does not help in increasing vocabulary, because the words used in poetry are generally not used in day-to-day life.

(v) The similes and metaphors used in poetry are beyond pupils understanding.

(vi) The foreign background described in poems is unfamiliar to Indian students.

The Aims of Teaching Poetry

The main aims of teaching poetry are:

(i) To enable pupils of lower classes to enjoy a poem.

(ii) To enable pupils of high and higher secondary classes to appreciate a poem, *i.e.*

(a) To appreciate the subject-matter,

(b) To appreciate the images that present the experience,

(c) To appreciate the music of rhyme and rhythm.

(d) To enable the pupils to develop their imagination and through that the very roots of mental life.

(e) Our aim's should be to give pleasure, and thus to lay foundation for an adequate appreciation of English poetry which may come latter.

(f) The poem should leave the child with a sense of satisfaction that comes from play, from absorption or from any spontaneous activity.

(g) The aim of teaching poetry is not so much to improve the child's knowledge of English as to add to his joy, and increase his power of appreciation of beauty.

Menon and Patel have said "the aim of teaching poetry is not so much to improve the child's knowledge of English as to add to his joy and increase his power of appreciation of beauty".

Methods of Teaching English Poetry

There is single method that can be used for the teaching of poetry. For teaching poetry, teachers should plan before hand. After making marginal entries, as in prose teaching, the following steps may be followed:

1. Aims

The main aim of teaching of poetry is to develop the power of appreciation of beauty.

General Aims

(i) To enable students to appreciate the beauty, rhyme and style of the poem.

(ii) To enable pupils to read the poem with proper rhythm and intonation.

(iii) To enable students to enjoy recitation, individual or chorus of the poem.

(iv) To make students understand the thought and imagination contained in the poem.

(v) To train the emotions of students.

(vi) To create a love for English literature in them.

(vii) To develop their aesthetic sense.

(viii) According to Rhyburn, "To give pleasure and thus to lay the foundation for an adequate appreciation of English poetry which may come latter".

(ix) According to Eastman, "To leave the child with a sense of satisfaction that comes from play, from absorption or from any spontaneous activity".

Specific Aims

The specific aims of teaching poetry differ from poem. They depend largely on situation, scene, feeling and thought depicted in the poem. Each poem brings a special and exclusive message from the poet. Nevertheless, the following are the specific aims of teaching any poem:

(i) To enable students to appropriate the poem namely "...........".

(ii) To enable students to read this poem with correct rhyme and rhythm.

(iii) To enable them to understand the idea of the poem, and

(iv) To communicate the pupils, the exclusive message of the poem.

2. Preparation

(a) Material aids : There is no need of material aids for teaching poetry. If the poetry is not making the scene clear, material aid of a picture depicting the scene is enough.

(b) Previous knowledge : The teacher should know the age, previous experiences and mental development of students. These help him in teaching the poetry, and linking the new knowledge to the previous one.

(c) Introduction : Before teaching the poem, the teacher should give an appropriate introduction to poem to arouse the interest of pupils, and to create the proper atmosphere for the poem. Introduction differs from poem to poem.

Thompson and Wyatt have suggested three ways of introduction:

(i) The best method is to read a parallel poem similar in subject-matter with the poem to be taught if possible, the parallel poem should be by the same poet.

(ii) Second method is to give the gist of poem, and then ask two or three simple questions on that.

(iii) The third method is to give the life sketch, style and characteristics of the poet.

Introduction can also be done as follows:

(i) Introduction can be done by playing some music.

(ii) The teacher can ask some questions on the previous knowledge of students.

(iii) If the poem to be learnt is descriptive, a picture can be shown. Two or three questions on picture should be asked.

Before introducing the poem, the teacher should give a short introductory talk either in the pupil's mother tongue or in simple English about the background on the general theme of the poem. This should be gone through quickly, lest the interest of students should flag. The introductory talk must have a bearing on the poem. Whatever method teacher employs for introduction, he should be particular about not to spoil the environment necessary for the poem.

(d) Statement of Aim : After making students curious to know about poem by introduction, the teacher should state the aim briefly in clear words.

3. Presentation

Ryburn says, "A good poem is a complete... whole" so the poetry should be taught in one unit with the following steps:

(a) Meaning of difficult words : Exposition and explanation are not done in teaching a poem. Then ask some difficult words in the poem, the teacher should tell their meaning one by one only orally. He should not give much time to it.

(b) Model recitation by the teacher : Students get pleasure from the poetry by its rhythm and musical sound. Therefore, the teacher should read the poem aloud. It may be done once, twice or thrice. This recitation of poetry by the teacher brings out clearly the beauty of sound and rhythm of thought and emotion, and the feelings of the poet when writing it. Ryburn rightly says, "A good poem should be taught whole". If, of course, it is very long, it should be divided into units.

(c) Loud reading by pupils : The teacher should ask two or three students to read the poem just as the teacher has read. The teacher should help them in reciting it with effect but not check them while reading, because it mars the flow.

(d) Silent reading by the pupils : Pupils should then be asked to read the poem silently, and try to grasp the general meaning. The students should be encouraged to bring their language difficulties to the notice of the teacher.

(e) Removal of language difficulties : The teacher should lose no time in dealing with difficult words, and a structure which stands in the way of student understanding, and enjoyment of the poem. The teacher should be selective and brief and he should concentrate only on those language items which are very essential.

(f) Final reading of the poem : As a last step, the students be asked to read the poem aloud in small groups or preferably individually. Great care should be exercised to ensure correct reading of the poem. As far as possible, the poem should be read as a whole.

4. Comprehension Questions

The purpose of such questions is to know if the meaning of poem is clear to students, and to make certain ideas are clear. These questions should be simple, and should not break the continuity of the poem. Their number depends upon the length and ideas of the poem.

5. Appreciation Questions

These questions aim to make clear the (i) beauty, (ii) feeling, and (iii) main idea of the poem. These questions are used to test:

(a) Appreciation of the beauty of thought,

(b) Appreciation of the beauty of images,

(c) Appreciation of the beauty of emotions, and

(d) Appreciation of the beauty of style and language.

6. Assignment

There is not much importance of assignment in poetry teaching. If teacher may ask the students to memorise the lines of the poem or to write the gist of the poem.

IX. Difference between Prose and Poetry

Prose and poetry are two different forms of literature. The points of difference between prose and poetry are as follows:

(i) Prose appeals to the head, while poetry appeals to the bean Butus' funeral, speech is in prose. It appeals to the head. Antony's speech is in verse. It appeals to bean.

(ii) Poetry appeals to the intellect only. It is more powerful form of expression. It affects the whole man, his sense, intellect and emotions.

(iii) Poetry is more sound than sight. It appeals principally to ear than eye. Prose is more sight than sound.

(iv) Unlike prose, poetry is not so much read but sung. Poetry is not so much seen it is heard. The poet uses music for the expression of his ideas. What distinguishes poetry from prose is that in poetry there is a peculiar rhythm that is not there in prose.

(v) Prose merely provides information, whereas poetry provides delight. Poetry is a thing of beauty, beauty of language, beauty of thought, beauty of mood and feeling. Poetry is for appreciation where as prose is for knowledge.

Differences in the aims of teaching prose and poetry

The aims of teaching poetry are quite different from those of teaching prose:

(i) Language skills: The aim of teaching poetry is not the development of language skill. The language skill is developed by teaching prose.

(ii) Acquire natural speech rhythm : Teaching of poetry at the early stage aims to help the learner acquire natural speech rhythm. However, the main aim of prose lesson is to enlarge the vocabulary, to explain the structure of sentences, and to enable the students to grasp the ideas and arguments of the author.

(iii) Impart pleasure to the students : The aim of teaching poetry is to impart pleasure to students by making them easily understand the thought, contents and feelings described in poem. It is to educate the pupil's emotions and increase their power of imagination.

(iv) Language practice: Unlike prose, poetry is not taught for language practice as this purpose can be better served by teaching prose.

(v) Natural speech rhythm : At an early stage, the aim of teaching of poetry is to help the learner natural speech rhythm, where as aim of teaching prose is to give understanding of new words, meanings, structures, etc.

Differences in Prose and Poetry Teaching

The major differences in prose and poetry teaching are:

(i) Prose is taught for language training and poetry teaching aims at appreciation of beauty.

(ii) In prose teaching, exposition and explanation are main priorities, where as in poetry teaching, it is not desirable, because it kills the aesthetic sense of the poem.

(iii) Poetry lesson is not taught in part like a prose lesson.

(iv) In poetry teaching, more emphasis is put on model reading than that on prose teaching.

(v) There is not much need of assignment in poetry teaching as it is in prose teaching.

X. Teaching of Vocabulary

The teacher can introduce the meaning of words through the different situations. We can make use of classroom situation, pictorial situation or verbal situation. We can show the objects to the children. Thus, the meaning of a word could be taught. This is called material association. The child associates the word with the object. This method is useful in the lower classes.

When real objects are not available or cannot be brought inside the classroom, models can be used to introduce a word. For example, ROCKET can be brought into the classroom. Here a model can be used.

With the help of pictures and charts we can introduce a word. This is the substitute for objects and models. When we cannot bring a railway engine into the classroom, we use pictures. Match stick figures and line drawing can be used to illustrate the meaning of words.

In order to explain certain words like sneezing and snoring, the teacher can demonstrate by action. Dramatisation can also be used to explain the meanings of words. We can also introduce the words through the following ways.

Using word categories

Stationary : Pen, Pencil, Book and Copy etc.

Utensils : Spoon, Cup, Plate and Saucer etc.

Using related words

A farm: Farmer, plough, seeds, fertiliser and harvest etc.

Definition

Parasite : Animal or plant living on or in another and getting its food from it.

Finding meaning from context

Experience/ Familiarity

Using Mother tongue

Using Antony in sentence context

Techniques of teaching vocabulary

The first step in teaching vocabulary is to determine the nature and the relative difficulty of the word. There are many words in English, which does not have exact translation equivalents. Most of the structural words and other high-frequency words come under this category.

(a) Actual objects or Models : Names of many things can be taught by showing the actual objects or these models, many inexpensive plastic models are available in the market, and the teacher should make frequent use of them.

(b) Actions : The meanings of many words can be made clear by performing simple actions in the classroom, e.g., walk, trot, and punch, etc.

(c) Pictures : The use of pictures for teaching meaning is quite obvious. Every good dictionary makes use of them. Any word can be taught with the help of a suitable picture.

(d) Blackboard sketches : A quick blackboard sketch may work wonders in teaching meaning. These sketches read not are very accurate or elaborate.

(e) Verbal content : These are many abstract words and meaning of them cannot be presented by visual means. With such words verbal content can be used.

(f) Illustrative sentences : An illustrative sentence is very helpful and every good dictionary makes use of such sentences. The teacher should come prepared with such sentences and use them after the pupils have grasped the general meaning of the word.

(g) Synonyms : If there is an acceptable synonym already known to the pupils, it can be used in sentences to teach the meaning of the new world.

(h) Antonyms : Like the synonym, antonym can also be used if the pupils already know it.

(i) Definition : The familiar practice of giving the definition of a word may also be found useful in some cases.

(j) Translation and explanation : These two seem to be the favourites of the teachers. But they are the least satisfactory means of teaching vocabulary. This should be done very sparingly.

Teaching of English Grammar and Translation

XI. Teaching of Grammar

Introduction

The general English course in our schools comprises 'Grammar and Translation'. So, the teacher should know about the teaching of grammar and translation. Every language has its grammar and the grammar of language is important because acceptability and intelligibility, both in writing and in speech depend on the currently followed basic notions and norms of grammar.

In order that we may decide for ourselves our approach to the study of grammar, we should know what 'Grammar' means to us.

What is Grammar?

The term 'grammar' has meant various things at various stages at various times and often several things at the same time.

In the eighteenth century Joseph Priestley, a well-known scientist, said, "Language is a method of conveying our ideas to the minds of other persons and the grammar of any language is a collection of observations on the structure of it, and a system of rules for proper use of it".

According to Chomsky, it is "simply a system of rules that in so explicit and well-defined way assign structural descriptions to sentences".

Dr Sweet has defined 'grammar' as "the practical analysis of the language and its anatomy".

Thompson and Wyatt observe, "Grammar presents the facts of language arranged under certain categories and deals only with what can be brought under general laws and stated in the form of general rules".

In the words of Dr West, "Grammar is not a code of rules; it is, like etiquette and table manners, a statement of convention; it summarises what is done by cultured people; and like etiquette, it is in a state of constant change".

Prof W.N. Fracis, "Grammar has three different meanings. The first meaning of 'grammar' — call it grammar 1—is the set of formal patterns in which the words of a language are arranged in order to convey larger meanings. The second meaning of grammar — call it grammar 2—is the branch of linguistic science which is concerned with the description, analysis and formalisation of formal language patterns. The third meaning of grammar — call it grammar 3—is linguistic etiquette.

Champion defines grammar as follows:

"Grammar is a study of language by specialists, made in order to establish the rules and principles which are followed more or less unconsciously by the native speakers".

These definitions of grammar lead us to the fact that grammar consists of certain rules and that it is these rules that govern the system of language units and structures by which we communicate with each other. Thus, the study of grammar can help us in communication as grammar is a system consisting of phonology, morphology, semantics and syntax.

Types of Grammar

Various types of grammar are:

(i) Perspective grammar,

(ii) Descriptive grammar,

(iii) Scholarly traditional grammar,

(iv) Structural grammar, and

(v) Transformational – generative grammar.

(i) Perspective Grammar : It is also known as formal or theoretical grammar. Its main emphasis is on rules and forms. Its limitation is that it does not consider 'change in language', whereas change in rules is must.

(ii) Descriptive Grammar : It is also known as functional grammar. Its main emphasis is on functional side of language. It changes along with the changes in the language.

(iii) Scholarly Traditional Grammar : It is developed by the scholars using bibliographic references, critical evolution of the work of predecessors, etc. The weakness of this type of grammar is diversity; therefore it did not influence the school of grammar.

(iv) Structural Grammar : It was founded by an American linguist C.C. Fries. It puts emphasis on the structure of sentences. The descriptive linguists are much influenced by it. But it is not a complete system.

One of the primary characteristics of structural grammar is its division of the study of language into two basic parts; structure and meaning. In general, the structural grammarian prefers to study the grammatical forms or structures of the language before considering lexical meaning. He feels that the opposite approach, used by traditional grammarians, interferes in the discovery of precisely how language works – that it keeps us from seeing that English is a system learnt by recognition of certain repeated grammatical signals. Structural grammar has been an innovative and important approach to the discovery of knowledge about English. Thus, it is called new grammar.

(v) Transformational – Generative Grammar : It considers sentences as of two types: (a) basic sentences, and (b) transformed sentences.

Basic sentences cannot be derived from other sentences whereas the transformed sentences are derived from the basic sentences.

Transformationalists do not consider grammar as description itself; they consider it as a particular theory that provides a complete, consistent explanation of the way a language operates. The theory explains and describes what is in existence and also predicts what will be.

The transformational – generative approach to grammar is characterised by abstraction. The components of this type of grammar are its, (i) phonological component, (ii) syntactic component, and (iii) semantic component. The exact relationship of these aspects is still unknown.

Merits and Demerits of Grammar

Advocating the cause of grammar L.A. Gordon says, "Language is the vehicle of our thoughts and feelings, and of our stories, whether true or not and grammar is the machinery by which that vehicle is set in motion".

Some of the merits of grammar are:

(i) For correct expression it is a must.

(ii) Grammar is behind the logic of a language.

(iii) To proceed from concrete to abstract grammar teaching is essential.

(iv) It provides an insight into the structure of the language.

(v) It is the systematised knowledge of the language.

(vi) Its importance in writing is undebatable.

(vii) It provides the criterion for judging the correctness of language.

(viii) It helps to develop various mental abilities such as reasoning, observation and concentrations.

(ix) It helps in writing correctly.

In the present times, grammar has been much criticised by the scholars. P. Gurrey views, "in secondary schools, the use of phrasing and full analysis is a waste of time compared to the effectiveness of many exercises".

Halliday *et al.,* condemn it by saying, "Much of English grammar taught with in the old method was pedantic, or archaic even erroneous".

According to Jesperson, "Grammar is not a set of stiff dogmatic percepts, according to which some things are correct and others absolutely wrong".

Some of the demerits responsible for the criticism of grammar are:

(i) Simply learning rules is not enough for language learning. Language learning is heavily dependent upon practice and habit formation, because it is a matter of skill.

(ii) The errors in language are not related to the knowledge of grammar. Kittson points out, "The notion that grammatical mistakes made by the learner are due to lack of grammatical knowledge is wholly false; this is often curiously illustrated in examinations which a candidate will not infrequently gain marks in one section of the paper by stating a grammatical rule correctly, and a little after he breaks the same rule in composition.

(iii) Knowledge of grammar never helps in either fluency of speech or articulation and colloquial expression.

(iv) It never provides ideas.

(v) According to Palmer, "it actually hinders the spontaneous learning of a foreign language".

(vi) In the view of Jesperson, "grammar has absured forms in it which are seldom used".

Place of Grammar in School Curriculum

In this confusion of differing approaches, theories, debates and discussions on the useful or otherwise of teaching of English grammar; what should be the standpoint of teacher of English in India? Certainly, he cannot do without grammar. As Wilkins observes, "the acquisition of the grammatical system of a language remains a most important element in language learning. The grammar is the means through which linguistic creativity is ultimately achieved and an adequate knowledge of the grammar would lead to serious limitations on the creativity for communication. A national syllabus, no less than a grammatical syllabus, must seek to ensure that grammatical system is properly assimilated by the learner". What Wilkins means is that grammar should be taught; without knowledge of grammar of the language, one's learning of the language is inadequate; conscious learning of grammar is slowly converted into an automatic process.

About the place and importance of grammar, Chapman has rightly opined, "the essential features of English which pupil must be acquainted with are: word order tense formation, sentence joints, the fixed nature of idioms and flexibility".

In modern curriculum grammar is given less importance. The place it should occupy should have following main features:

(i) The descriptive grammar which puts emphasis on function of language should be taught. According to Ballard, "formal grammar fails to provide a general mental training, does not enable teacher to eradicate error, does not aid in composition and takes up time which could much more profitably be devoted to the study of literature".

(ii) It should be taught incidentally and informally at the early stage.

(iii) It should occupy a secondary place.

(iv) It should follow the language. C.E. Eckersely says, "the rules of grammar are like the laws of nature. The laws were not made for nature to obey, but are simply a few facts which wise men have observed as to the way nature acts. So the grammarian merely examines the language of best speakers and writers and deduces rules from their use of it."

(v) Teaching of grammar should only start when pupils acquire some command over the language.

(vi) During the first year only function of words, and the way they are used should be taught. During the second year and the third year, sentence pattern, phrase pattern, structural words and the ways in which English uses a few inflexions should be taught. At the senior stage, these should be followed coupled with analysis, synthesis, direct and indirect narration, transformation, compound and difficult sentences.

Distinction between Formal and Functional Grammar

Formal grammar lays stress on form rather than function, on definition rather than on their application, teachers teach the rules and students are expected to learn these by heart. There is also a prescribed text-book. No emphasis is laid on the verbal expression. Students only know the grammatical rules but do not know how to apply them. Thus, grammar is taught for the sake of grammar. Now, it has been realised that the most important aspect of any language learning is not grammar but the sentence structure.

Functional grammar does not emphasise the form or the rules of grammar, but the function of the word in a particular context. It classifies words according to their functions and asserts that there is no grammatical classification of certain words. It implies that whatever pupils learn, they should use it immediately in real and written composition. Functional grammar is strongly supported because of its practical value.

Methods of Teaching Grammar

Once it is admitted that teaching grammar is necessary; how is it to be taught?

Some of the methods used for the teaching of grammar are:

1. The Traditional Method,
2. The Informal Method,
3. The Reference or Correlation Method, and
4. The Inductive-Deductive Method.

1. The Traditional Method

This method takes help of a grammar book for teaching the grammar. The book contains various rules, definitions, etc., and the teacher tries to make clear these to the students by citing suitable examples. This method suffers from the following limitations :

(a) It emphasises cramming.

(b) It is against the educational maxims, "proceed from simple to complex" and "proceed from known to unknown".

(c) Students find it least interesting.

This method is almost obsolete now.

2. The Informal Method

It advocates the teaching of grammar not by rules but by usages. By continuously using words while speaking, reading and writing, grammar can be learnt. This method is quite useful at the early stages. This method suffers from following limitations.

(a) All rules cannot be taught by this method.

(b) Students do not get systematised knowledge of grammar.

(c) It consumes much tune and labour of students.

3. The Reference or Correlation Method

It is also called incidental method, since in this method, grammar is taught incidentally, while teaching the text-book, translating a passage or doing composition, the teacher explains the grammatical rules, complex structures as also their implications. It is also called reference or correlation method because grammar is taught by relating it to text-book translation and composition. It suffers from the following limitations :

(a) It is not a complete method.

(b) It can interface with the normal teaching.

4. The Inductive-deductive Method

It is considered as the best method, because it follows certain educational principles.

Inductive means to proceed from observation to law and deductive means to proceed from law to observation. To teach grammar by this method, following steps are to be followed:

Inductive Process

(i) Present some examples,

(ii) Observe and analyse the examples, and

(iii) Generalise.

Deductive Process

(i) Verification and application of rule,

(ii) Practice.

Merits of the Method

(i) It follows certain educational principles, e.g., "from known to unknown", "from simple to complex", "from concrete to abstract", etc.

(ii) Pupils remain active.

(iii) Pupils find it interesting.

(iv) In it cramming is not needed.

(v) It develops the power of reasoning, and thinking in the students.

(vi) According to P.C. Wren, "Teach grammar inductively, teaches English as you would, by action and practice. The rules show themselves in both and need not be learnt fast. Not should a boy be able to define a foot-ball or cricket-ball, before he can play with one. Why should we define a noun or a verb before he can use one".

Demerits of the Method

It has the following demerits:

(i) It can be applied usefully only at an early stage.

(ii) It is not full in itself.

Choice of Method

A good teacher should be eclectic. He need not accept any one theory in tow; he should select what is best suited for his purpose in the classroom. He need not have a whole-hearted commitment to traditional grammar; nor should be reject outright the insights of modern linguistics. He should explain and describe the grammatical aspects of structures, illustrate them with examples and lay down certain rules for his students' guidance and practice. In other words, he should have his own approach based on a synthesis of the insight, he has acquired from his study of different approaches to the teaching of grammar.

XII. Teaching of Translation

We can use translation either as a teaching method or as a skill. Translation as a teaching method has been condemned. As a skill, it has its own importance. The translation skill involves a high-level of understanding of one language, and a good command of the other.

Types of Translation

(i) Word translation,

(ii) Sentence translation.

Both these can be:

(i) From English to mother-tongue,

(ii) From mother-tongue to English.

Another classification could be:

(i) Oral translation,

(ii) Written translation.

Exercise for Translation

(i) Structures, and

(ii) Sentences with:

(a) Different tenses,

(b) Relative pronouns,

(c) Comparative and superlative degrees,

(d) Active and passive voices,

(e) Direct and indirect narrations,

(f) Appropriate prepositions,

(g) Words like however, although, nevertheless, yet, though, notwithstanding, etc.

(iii) Idioms and phrases, and

(iv) Passages.

Significance of Translation

(i) It serves as exercise in comprehension.

(ii) It helps the teacher to test the understanding of the pupil of an English word. According to Ryburn, "there is no better test of knowledge of English than translation from the mother-tongue into English".

(iii) It brings out the difference of grammatical structures of sentences in English and mother-tongue.

(iv) There is much need of translation of books on humanities and science. For this purpose, translation skill is quite useful.

(v) It makes students learn English by understanding its differences from the mother-tongue.

(vi) In the opinion of R.N. Tagore, ".... If we give them a passage from a good English author, and ask them to translate it, the inherent difference between the two languages becomes quite evident from the very beginning. Now, when they translate it back into English, they naturally follow the Bengali form and at that time if his English is corrected by carefully comparing it with the original passage, the peculiarities of English style will effectively be impressed on the minds of the pupils".

Due to this significance, Gibbon calls it an excellent method. According to Champion, "Something of a great value will have been lost, if the pupils are not trained in the different arts of rendering one language into another".

Therefore, as said by Mr French "Translation cannot be completely shut out from the English lesson".

Some Useful Suggestions for Teaching of Grammar and Translation

Teaching of Grammar

(i) The Idson should be planned before hand.

(ii) The material should be taken from text-book.

(iii) The method of teaching should be chosen keeping in view the age and general standard of students.

(iv) Appropriate material aids should be used e.g., pictures, flash-cards, and substitution tables.

(v) Sufficient spoken and written work is essential.

(vi) The teacher should be particular about the written work.

(vii) For evaluation, objective type tests should be used.

Teaching of Translation

(i) Material for translation should be properly selected and graded.

(ii) Literal translation should be avoided.

(iii) Comparison and contrast in the pattern of two languages should be emphasised.

(iv) The sentences and passages for translation should be according to the vocabulary and knowledge of grammar of students.

(v) When new words are introduced they should be helped with a glossary.

(vi) Translation of ideas should be stressed.

XIII. TEXT BOOKS

Introduction

Text-books occupy an important place during primary and secondary education. In English teaching, text-books are all the more important. R.S. Trivedi rightly observes, "In the absence of any other instructional material, the text-book becomes a potent book in the hands of a teacher to teach the skill of a language and theoretical language". . Text-book is the most widely used teaching instrument. It is not merely a source of information but a course of study, a set of unit plans, and a learning guide. It helps to revise and reinforce the language material already taught. The teacher must be able to evaluate the text-book he has to use. For this, teacher must know the criterion of a text-book.

Importance of English Text-book

(i) It makes the teaching of English systematic.

(ii) It presents in concrete form the limited portion of the language to be taught in a given time.

(iii) It checks the teachers from going astray.

(iv) It facilitates and stabilises student's learning.

(v) It helps students in self-study.

(vi) It gives examples of the ways in which certan items of vocabulary, and structure can be taught. Such examples are quite helpful to students.

(vii) It also serves as an index for academic achievement.

(viii) It serves as a memory aid for teachers.

(ix) It helps in supplementing pupils learning experiences.

Emphasising the importance of text - books Billows says, "to make the best use of time in the classroom, and to avoid unintended repetition or the neglect of essential language patterns, the teacher is wise to have a text - book, at least in the background of his mind".

Advantages of Text-books

(i) They are cheap and economical,

(ii) They facilitate individual instructions,

(iii) They organise and provide uniformity for class instructions,

(iv) They stimulate active learning,

(v) They develop the skill of teachers, and

(vi) They stimulate self-directed activities of the students.

Characteristics of a Good Text Book in English

Following characteristics are desirable in a good English text-book:

(i) Adequate Subject Matter

(a) It should be according to psychological needs and requirements of the child.

(b) It should be related to pupils' environment.

(c) It should have a link with the Indian culture and tradition.

(d) It should have varied topics.

(e) It should be of practical utility as well as informative.

(ii) Pictures and Illustrations

(a) It should have illustrations.

(b) Pictures and illustrations should be relevant and correct to the nature of topic of the lesson.

(c) These should be attractive and clear.

(d) Some of them be presented in colours.

(iii) Opportunity of Oral Work

(a) It should provide sufficient opportunity for oral work.

(b) The lessons should be based on the possibility of introductory oral work.

(iv) Suitable Vocabulary and Structures

(a) The vocabulary should be controlled. According to the All India Council for Secondary Education, it should contain 2,500 words and 250 structures for six - year course of English.

(b) The vocabulary should be properly selected and graded.

(c) The introduction of vocabulary should be progressive within the series of readers.

(d) The word pattern, phrase pattern and sentence pattern or structure should also be selected and graded carefully.

(e) A new word or pattern must be repeated.

(f) Sufficient pattern practice be provided through sufficient exercises.

(v) Developing Language Skill

It should provide necessary facilities for developing the necessary language skills of speaking, reading and writing in the young learners.

(vi) Style

(a) The style should be based on the principle of 'Simple to Complex'.

(b) The subject matter should be presented in a logical manner.

(c) The style should be appealing to the students.

(vi) Contents

(a) It should contain sufficient and suitable teaching and testing exercises on each lesson.

(b) The content and the language material in each lesson should be further practiced and tested through a variety of interesting and graded exercises at the end of each lesson.

(c) The instructions for each exercise should be simple enough for students to understand.

(viii) Cultural Content

(a) A good text book in English must also contain cultural content about the regions of India.

(b) Some of the lessons must also be based on English life.

(c) Suitable pictures be given to illustrate such lessons.

(ix) Technical Characteristics

(a) The paper used should be white and durable.

(b) The print should be attractive with no mistakes.

(c) The size of the type should be bold for juniors and small for seniors.

(d) Symmetry, margin and spacing should be proper.

(e) The headings and sub-headings should be in a very bold type.

(f) It should be bound properly.

(g) The cover should be thick and durable with some interesting illustration over it.

(h) A jacket should be added to the cover.

(i) The book should be handy. It should have quartz size for junior class and crown size for senior class.

(j) It should be moderately priced.

(x) Teacher's Hand-book

A good text book of English should be supplemented by teacher's hand-book. It will guide the teachers. Teaching of English can be made more effective and useful and the teachers can go a long way in the improvement of linguistic attainment of the students with the help of teacher's Hand-book.

XIV. Teaching of English Composition

An expression of ideas in English is one of the objectives of English teaching. Thompson and Wyatt are of the view, "the power of expression in a language, in a matter of skill rather than of knowledge".

Speech is the beginning of the all language learning. In face to face communication speech is the best choice. But, when the conveyer and the receiver of the message are not physically present and there is no other means (telephonic facility) to establish verbal link between the two, written forms is the only choice. So, writing symbols were invented out of necessity of man. To write means to put down the graphic symbols of the language. Mere putting down the symbols, or sketching them on paper, etc., is not writing unless the writer understands the symbols of the language he is writing.

Meaning and Definition of Composition

The process of writing is divided into four stages: structuring, copying, transcribing and composition. Structuring requires teaching the child how to write the letters of the alphabet. The student has to be shown where to begin each letter, which side to move and how to connect the strokes and the letters. This can be taught with the help of arrows. When the students acquire sufficient practice to write the letters of the alphabet automatically without any difficulty, the next step is that of copying. Students should be encouraged to copy large pieces of the material that they have read in their text-books. Transcribing is a more advanced practice than copying. This includes the practice of writing without any help of the text. Composition is a further advantaged stage of learning to write on some topics of interest in a systematic way. Simple story writing, essay writing, letter writing, dialogue writing, etc., can be some of the forms of composition. Proper organisation, clarity and effectiveness of the subject-matter are some of the important points that should be kept in mind by the students while writing composition as its main theme is to communication in an organised way.

Bhatia and Bhatia has defined composition as, "it is the expression of child's thoughts, his own ideas, feelings and observations. It includes both the process and product of composing. It refers to the process of collecing thoughts, arranging them in a rational sequence, and ultimately expressing them in accordance with reorganised standards of form. The product may take the shape of a letter, an application, a paragraph, a story, an essay, a description or narration, a poem, etc".

Prerequisites for teaching composition: The prerequisites for teaching compositions are as follows:

(1) Students should have a fair knowledge of English language. This involves the knowledge of sufficient English vocabulary, structures and spellings. The students should be able to speak, read and write English.

(2) They must have sufficient ideas.

(3) They should have their mental devleopment of the level that they can arrange ideas in a sequence.

Characteristics of Composition: The following are the main features of composition :

1. It is fourth or last stage of writing process.

   (a) Structuring, (b) Copying, (c) Transcribing, and (d) Composition.

2. Composition is an advanced stage of learning or writing process even without any help of the text.

3. Composition is the expression of students' thoughts, ideas, feelings, observations, experiences in written form.

4. Composition refers to the process of collecting thoughts or information, arranging them in a sequence and expresses them in accordance with recognised standard form.

5. Composition is the process as well as product. The product may take the shape of a letter, an application, a story, an essay, a poem, a description or narration, etc.

6. Composition means to write on some topic of his own interest in a systematic way. Simple essay writing, story writing, letter writing, dialogue writing, writing a poem, etc., are some of the forms of composition.

7. Composition is the proper organisation. Clarity and effectiveness of the subject-matter are some of the important points or the theme are kept in mind while writing composition.

8. The composition, the main theme is communicated in an organised an systematic order.

The Objective of Teaching Composition

The following are some of the objectives of teaching composition:

1. To encourage the students to express their ideas in writing in an organised and systematic way.

2. To communicate information that could be followed readily by the intended reader.

3. To enable the students to arrange their ideas in writing at a reasonable speed and with accuracy.

4. To enable them to recall appropriate vocabulary and use it in sentences.

5. To enable them to make use of appropriate punctutaion marks for clarity of ideas.

6. To enable them to fix the structures and vocabulary already learnt by them orally.
7. To develop among students the communicative competence through writing.

Principles of Teaching Composition

Some important principles of teaching composition are given below:

1. ***Principle of Proper Selection:*** Only such topics should be selected as are of interest. Topics should be meaningful and experience based.
2. ***Principle of Gradation:*** It implies that the selection of topics should be made in accordance with the age, ability and class-level of the students.
3. ***Principle of Utility:*** The topics selected for composition should be related to day to day life of the students.
4. ***Principle of Group Involvement*:** The composition work should involve the whole class, so that group thinking could take place. The involvement of all classmates in thinking will help the students to exchange their views and suggest new ideas through mutual discussion.
5. ***Principle of Oral Practice:*** Oral-Composition-Practice should be given to students before asking them to write anything. This will reduce the chances of doing mistakes in the written work.
6. ***Principle of Sequence*:** The subject-matter should have some sequence. It should not look disconnected collection of ideas.
7. ***Principles of Timely Correction:*** The written work of students should be corrected within reasonable time limit otherwise students will carry the mistakes with them till the time of correction.
8. ***Principle of Follow Up:*** After knowing the difficulties and problems of students, the teacher should find suitable remedial measures to remove their difficulties and mistakes.

Types of Composition and their teaching: There are two types of composition: (i) Oral and (2) Written. These are two types of each; (1) guided and (2) free. This can be shown by the following diagram.

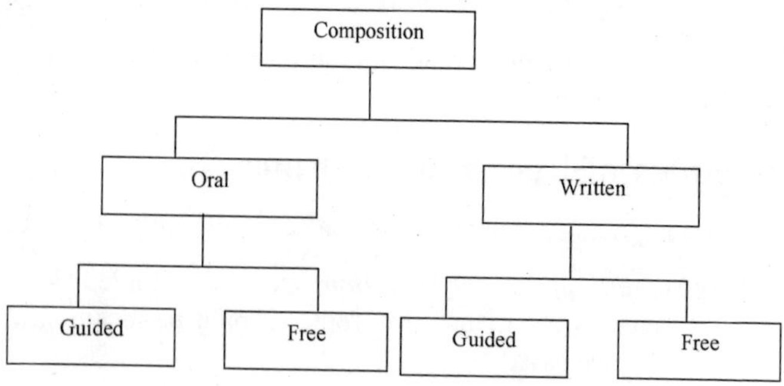

We shall come to know about these one by one.

Oral Composition

Oral composition is of immense importance, as is clear by Laurie's remark, "The habit or oral composition should be kept up during the whole school period". It should always precede written composition. Composition should begin with the power of speech and should be oral long before it is written.

Objects of oral composition: The following are the objective of oral composition.

(i) To give practice in using the English language.

(ii) To make pupils express their interests, feelings, ideas, needs and knowledge of English language.

(iii) To promote a clear thinking.

Teaching of oral composition: In the following manner, the teacher can teach oral composition to students at the early stage.

a) Asking students to produce sentences which he speaks, e.g.,

Teacher : I am writing.

Pupil : I am writing.

b) The teacher asks a few questions about some object or some activity. For instance,

Teacher : What is that?

Pupil	:	That is a black-board.
Teacher	:	What is this?
Pupil	:	This is a chalk.
Teacher	:	What am I doing?
Pupil	:	You are writing on the black-board.

(c) Giving commands to students for execution, e.g., open the window; write on the black-board.

(d) Asking students to read a substitution table like this one:

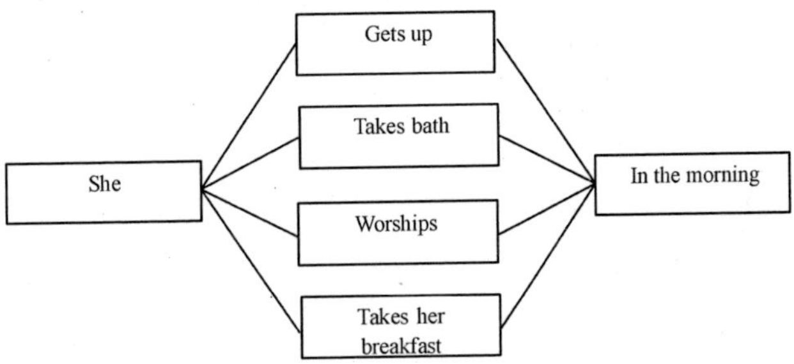

Then, they may be asked to substitute the table with other suitable words, e.g., substitute the words in the second column.

(e) Asking questions on a picture after describing that, e.g.,

Teacher	:	Who is he?
Pupil	:	He is Denu.
Teacher	:	What is he doing?
Pupil	:	He is bathing.
Teacher	:	Who is she?
Pupil	:	She is Denu's sister.
Teacher	:	What is she doing?
Pupil	:	She is washing clothes.

(f) Asking questions from the textbook.

(g) Initiating conversation with pupils and among pupils on simple topics.

(h) Narrating simple stories and asking students to give the gist.

(i) Asking students to play simple short dramas.

The teaching of oral composition at later stage should be by the following exercises.

(a) Reproduction of stories,
(b) Description of objects and pictures,
(c) Conversation,
(d) Dialogue,
(e) Debate,
(f) Dramatisation,
(g) Speeches, and
(h) Description of incidents.

Significance of Oral Composition: The following are the points showing the significance of oral composition:

(i) It is simple and saves time.
(ii) It forms the foundation for written composition.
(iii) It develops speaking ability.
(iv) Students find it interesting.
(v) It helps students to think clearly.
(vi) According to Grenning, "Oral exercises are still the best means of getting good results. Writing is at the best a slow and laborious process and while a boy is writing one sentence, he could say a dozen and so get a correspondingly greater practice in expressing his ideas".

Written composition is divided into two types – Guided and Free.

2. Guided Composition

Guided composition is also known as controlled or directed

composition. Pupils are supplied with the necessary vocabulary and structures to be used for expressing the desired thoughts and ideas in writing. The teacher guides the students what to write and how to write with the help of controlled vocabulary and structural words. Actually guided compositions are those written exercises in which utterances are already known to the students orally but they are asked to write them down. It should, however, be noted that the nature of the language control should be such that it would allow a gradual relaxation of control, so that students could proceed from controlled composition to free composition. Even in controlled composition exercises the aim should be left free to use the words and structures in language of their own. The aim should be to give direction and not to put restrictions. The job of the teacher is to make necessary correction in the composition. If the attempt of the students is correct, he may be encouraged to proceed to the next step and if there are mistakes in it, he is asked to repeat the same step by giving him proper direction.

The common objection to guided composition is that it is mechanical for the students. Unless the student understands what he is going to write, it is likely to result in an incorrect composition. Another charge against this is that it curtails freedom of the students. To quote Allen & Campbell 'guided composition is not a panacea for all the problems of teaching composition to foreign students. There is still much that needs further exploration and experimentation.

At the early stage the composition whether oral or written should be strictly guided, because pupils should proceed from imitation to improvisation, from reproduction or original expression. Oral or written composition are guided when,

(i) The topic for the composition is carefully selected by the teachers.

(ii) The various details of the topic are given to students by the teachers.

(iii) The teacher also decides the procedure for the practical completion of the topic.

(iv) The vocabulary and structure to be used is thought over by the teacher.

(v) The teacher is always ready to guide students in the composition work.

Guided composition can be done by the following exercises:

(a) Substitution tables,

(b) Transcription,

(c) Dictation, and

(d) Transformation of sentences, e.g.,

She is walking (change the gender),

He is walking (change into past tense),

She is walking,

(e) Composition of incomplete sentence, and

(f) Reproduction.

(i) Reproducing a situation, e.g., the teacher says, "This is a table. I am putting a book on it. The book is mine". Then students will be asked to reproduce by replacing book with some other object.

(ii) Reproducing a picture description.

(iii) Reproducing answers, and

(iv) Reproducing a story.

Merits of Guided composition:

The following are the merits:

(i) Guided composition paves the way for free composition.

(ii) The teacher can correct the mistakes of students at the very begining.

(iii) The assistance of teacher makes composition writing for little children interesting.

(iv) Guided composition also corrects grammatical mistakes, and

(v) Students learn structures too.

3. Free Composition

In guided composition, students are required to compose the actual utterances of which they possess a clear idea when they write with the help of guidance. As the students gain mastery over the language, the guidance is gradually reduced, and they are encouraged to write freely on their own. Here, they are free to use vocabulary and structures of their own for expressing their own views and thoughts related to a given topic. This is known as free composition. It is also called creative or imaginative writing. It may include writing of essays, stories, descriptions, etc. Originality, accuracy and proper organisation of the subject-matter are its important considerations. This should be the ultimate aim of teaching composition which is rather a difficult one to achieve because English is taught as a second language, and it requires a lot of practice to write correct English. So, the teacher should not be over-eager to make his students switch over to free composition until they acquire sufficient proficiency in the language. At the school stage, most of the writing is of the 'guided nature' and sufficient control is introduced in the early stages. But as soon as students reach higher classes, the control is progressively reduced and students are given freedom to use new words of their choice.

French correctly states, " Free composition in which the child has to make-up his own thoughts, has no place in the first three years of a six or seven years course. If it is used, it will only result in a large number of most discouraging mistakes". A free composition is in which:

(i) There are no restrictions on pupils for use of vocabulary and structure.

(ii) There are no restrictions on the length of composition.

(iii) Pupils are free to tackle the topic set for them, and

(iv) Pupils are forced to think freely.

H. Champion says, "The ultimate aim of composition is to enable the pupil to arrange his own ideas in his own way, freely; to choose his own words; to express his own ideas, freely. Hence, the terms 'free composition".

TYPES OF FREE COMPOSITION: There are nine important types of free composition:

1. Paragraph construction,
2. Narrative writing,
3. Paraphrasing,
4. Letter writing,
5. Application writing,
6. Essay waiting
7. Descriptive writing,
8. Story writing, and
9. Precis writing

1. Paragraph construction

Just as a sentence is formed out of words, so is a paragraph formed out of sentences. But just as a mere collection of words without any clear meaning is not a sentence, so also a mere juxtaposition or collection of sentences is not a paragraph. Paragraph is a unit of composition in any connected piece of writing which represents a logical organisation of ideas or thoughts. A long piece of composition may have many paragraphs.

For example, if we write an essay on a horse, we can write many paragraphs, describing in the first, the appearance of the horse, in the second its habits and in the last its usefulness. All the three paragraphs are on horse, but take separately, each is on one aspect of the horse and each paragraph is complete in itself. From this example, we can easily infer that the most essential requirement of a paragraph is the unity of the sentences related to the subject. But unity is not all. A good paragraph should also be coherent, that is the sentences in it should be arranged in an orderly way.

Technique of writing a paragraph: A good paragraph is a structured, whole representing a logical arrangement of ideas. The central idea of a paragraph is usually drawn from a sentence that may occur anywhere in the paragraph. The following points should be carefully notes while writing a paragraph.

1. **Mutual relationship of sentences should be maintained**: The most common practice for this is to use certain conjunctions, adverbs or other connectives.
2. **Emphasis on important points should be given**: This can be done by treating the important idea at greater length than the less important ideas. The important statements should occupy the central place in the paragraph.
3. **The theme of a paragraph ought to receive emphasis**: The beginning is the most prominent place for the theme to be mentioned. The sentence that depicts the theme is called the 'Tropical Sentence', i.e., the sentence that states the topic or theme of the paragraph. But it is not essential that topical sentence may occur in every case. In narrative or descriptive paragraphs, it is difficult to put the matter of the entire paragraph into a topical sentence.
4. Apart from these internal organisations, there are some signals

to indicate that the new paragraph is intended to give a new point of view related to the topic. That's why the beginning and the end of a paragraph are separated by leaving blank spaces, so that it begins a little space away from the left hand side and leaves enough blank space at the concluding right hand side.

5. Regarding the length of a paragraph, no hard and fast rule can be laid down. Some writers are fond of writing long paragraphs. In 'The History of King Richard the Third' of Sir Thomas More (1478-1535), there is a paragraph of about 1,000 words. Writers, today favour short, simple paragraphs. Much depends on the subject matter, and on the habit of the writer. In descriptive writing, the paragraphs are supposed to be long.

6. The mutual relationship of paragraphs is another important point to be noted. Just as the sentence is a part of the paragraph, so is a paragraph a part of a big composition. Mutual relation of the paragraphs must be maintained. Transition from one paragraph to another should be indicated by single words or phrases of sentences like 'more over', 'further more', 'meanwhile', 'hence', 'as we have seen', etc., etc.

It is necessary that the teacher himself should be efficient in the art of paragraph writing. Sufficient practice should be given to the students at the school stage on paragraphing.

2. Paragraphing

Paragraphing is different from paragraph writing. To paraphrase is to express the meaning of a passage in one's own different words. It is like translating one style of expression into another in the same language. But it does not mean just changing the wording, but it aims at explaining its meaning and interpreting it in clear language. Passages of poetry are interpretated in prose. Paraphrasing has another advantage. It adds to the students' vocabulary, because they are required to find suitable synonyms for difficult words.

Procedure of Paraphrasing: The following points should be carefully noted:

1. The passage should be read carefully in order to find out its complete sense.
2. All difficult expressions must be paraphrased in other simple

words and meaning of the passage should be expressed as accurately as possible.

3. No fresh idea should be introduced in paraphrasing.
4. The order in which the ideas occur in the original passage should, as far as possible, be maintained in the paraphrase.
5. Word by word paraphrasing should not be done. But no idea should be omitted.
6. Normally, a passage should not be made short in a paraphrase, nor should it be expanded too much.
7. Interpretation, fullness, unity and readability are the qualities of a good paraphrase.

3. Letter Writing

Letter writing is a gentle art. Letters are meant not merely to convey information, but to communicate the pleasant warmth of friendliness. Letter writing is a commonly taught form of composition at a school level. But it is not easy to write a poem. Our Indian students often find it difficult to write a letter in English.

A good letter must be simple because the aim is not to show one's scholarship and command over English, but it should reveal one's personality. Its style should be attractive without being showy.

Classification of Letters

We can arbitrarily classify letters into three classes:

1. Friendly letters including personal letters.
2. Business letters.
3. Social letters – invitations, replies, etc.

Procedure of writing a letter

1. The writer should write his address at the right hand side of the top of the page.
2. The date should be put immediately under the address, thus:

21, Shanti Nagar, Jaipur (Raj)

September 10, 1993

3. The opening salutation should begin from the left hand side. All relatives should be addressed as 'My dear –'. The relationship with elders must be indicated as 'My dear Father', or 'My dear Mother'. Younger ones may be addressed by their names.

4. Friends should be addressed 'My dear —' or 'Dear –", thus: My dear Mohan, or Dear Mohan.

5. Acquaintances should be addressed as 'My dear –' or 'Dear Miss —, or 'Dear Mrs.'...

6. Strangers should be addressed as 'Sir' or 'Dear sir' or 'Dear madam'.

7. The body of the letter should not be bookish. Its style should be simple and conversational. Humour is most welcome in a friendly letter. But in business letters the style should not be characterised by humour. Brevity, clarity and consciseness are the qualities of a good business letter.

8. In letters to relatives, the subscription should be – 'yours affectionately' or 'Your most affectionate son', (or) 'brother', (or) 'sister' etc.

In letters to friends, the subscription should be 'yours sincerely'. In case of acquaintances, we can write 'yours truly' or 'yours very truly'. The letters to teachers should end with 'Yours obediently' or 'yours respectfully'.

9. The closing lines may be like these:

   (i) With best wishes,

   (ii) With kind regards,

   (iii) With affectionate regards,

   (iv) Looking forward to bearing from you,

   (v) With love.

10. Social letters should also be polite like the business letters. In invitation letters, care should be taken not to write unnecessary matter which has nothing to do with the invitation. It is different from a regular letter. Sometimes letters of invitation are written in third person such as:

'The members of the English Literary Society request the pleasure of Dr.... at a tea party to be arranged at .... On Monday the 15th August, at 5.30 pm.,

The Secretary,

English Literary Society,

Ganganagar (Raj.)

11. If it is an invitation to a tea or dinner, there should be an R.S.V.P. at the bottom of the letter which stands for 'Respondez s'il vous plait' meaning 'Reply if you please'.

As a matter of fact, the real problem is realised in guiding the pupils to write freely. This requires a lot of individual attention by the teacher. A resourceful teacher can encourage his class by a variety of ways. He may ask the students to think different sentences that they would like to write to their friends related to a particular point or event. In this way, different responses can be obtained from the students. Necessary correction can be made in them by the teacher. This can create interest among students for letter writing.

4. Application Writing

Application writing comes under the category of business letters which include (a) Official letters; (b) Applications; (c) Letters to Newspapers, and (d) Ordinary business correspondence.

Application should begin with 'Sir' to address the officer concerned. The starting lines can begin with such lines as – 'I respectfully beg to state' or 'in response to your advertisement dated.... I beg to offer myself as a candidate'. The body of the application must furnish the required information in a systematic way. The concluding lines can be any of the following:

(a) Hoping a favourable consideration,

(b) Thanking you in anticipation.

Applications for a job should end with – yours faithfully, followed by a comma. Similarly, the applications to the Headmasters/Principals should conclude with – yours obediently. This subscription is suitable for students only. Parents of students need not write 'yours obediently'. They can use — yours faithfully.

The teacher should encourage his students to begin from simple applications to be addressed to the Headmasters/Principal of their school requesting for the solutions of their problems related to any school area. Thereafter, they should be guided how to write other types of applications.

5. Essay Writing

It is an important form of free composition in which the students give a proof of their language ability as well as their ability to observe keenly and attentively. The students of higher classes should be helped to write descriptive essays like 'An Indian Village', narrative essays like 'A House on Fire', reflective essays like 'Friendship', expository essays like 'The Uses of Science' and simple argumentative and imaginative essays like 'Village Life vs Town Life' and "If I were the Chief Minister of the State', etc.

6. Descriptive Writing

Description may deal with any object, organs of sense and states of mind to which objects, acts and ideas may give rise. Description has been defined as the enumeration of certain details that go to make up an object. We have to describe so many things and events to others in our day to day life. When we describe ordinarily, we do it casually in a haphazard way, but descriptive writing is an art which has to be learnt.

The Technique of Description: When a student wants to describe something in writing, he should bear the following steps in mind:

1. **Observation and collection of facts:** If you are going to describe an object, observe all its features carefully. For collection of facts, careful observation of things is very essential. All great descriptive writers possessed seeing eye. The observation should be close, full and accurate. The important facts observed by you should be noted down on a paper.

2. **Proper selection:** Everything that is observed cannot be described, because it will make the description too long and flat. One has to select the significant characteristics of the observed material. Suppose, we have to describe a postman. The bag that he carries and the uniform that he wears are chief characteristics of him. So, the most relevant and striking features need description.

3. **Proper arrangement:** Proper arrangement in language is the next step. A good descriptive writing depends on its arrangement. There should be some system – i.e., from head to foot or from foot to head.

4. **Proper language:** Language is the soul of description. Precision is very important to make the description impressive and clear. A student may not possess a Milton's aptitude for epic simile, but he can do well without similies.

5. **Proper form of description:** Descriptions can be made either in the first person or in the third person. Both are good at their own places. Students should practice both the methods. In short, fullness, vividness, and clarity are the qualities of a good descriptive writing.

7. Narrative Writing

The boundary line between narration and description is very thin. It is said that we narrate an event and describe an object. The main difference between the two is that narration the writer moves from point to point in time and in description, he moves from point to point in space. In other words, in narration one has to deal with particular things and represent them as moving from one point in time to another point of time. For example, I want to narrate an event of theft. At first, I shall narrate the events that happened when the thief entered the room, and then I shall deal with the incidents that took place after his entry and lastry, I shall deal with what happened-after he left the room. So, this is called movement from point to point in time. But when we are to describe something about a building or a movement, we move from point to point in space.

The technique of Narrative Writing: Narrative writing is an art. The following steps should be observed carefully for a good narrative work:

1. **Plot:** Plot is the first requisite of a narrative. If there is a plot, there can be a beginning, a middle and end. So, plot is very essential for movement of ideas.

2. **Movement:** The story moves from one point to another. Movements are those incidents which provide an attractive turn to the story. In other words, movements are series of situations in a story that are unstable and compel the actors to move on.

3. **Order:** It includes an orderly arrangement of events. Orderliness

develops interest of the reader. The order should end at climax, which is the attractive goal desired by the readers.

4. **Some description is also essential:** Though, much description may create hindrance, one cannot go without description. Description makes the story colourful and interesting provided it is not long. Dialogues can also be introduced wherever necessary.

8. Story Writing

Narrative writing also includes the development of stories out of bare outlines. Students are given the bare outlines of a story, and asked to make a complete story out of it. The students should read the given hints of the story carefully, and try to fill in the gaps by giving details of the relevant possible incidents. Main points should be noted down on a paper giving proper order to the major points of the story. After the story has become clear, they should begin writing the story. It must be noted that the outline gaps are not to be filled in by one or two words. It is not a 'fill in the blank' exercise. The gaps are to be completed by giving full details.

The students can be asked to write a complete story with the help of the outlines. This is a difficult thing to do because it requires a logical thinking on the part of students. What a student is expected to write must be consistent with the hints given in the outlines. Sometimes incomplete outlines are given and students are asked to complete the story with the help of incomplete hints. Here, the remaining part of the story is to be thought out by the students. This is rather a difficult job to do as compared to the complete outlines given for making the story.

Sometimes students are given to write a story illustrating a proverb. The procedure for it is that they should think over the proverb and find out its exact meaning. The story should illustrate the proverb.

9. Precis Writing

Précis is just a summary. It may be the summary of a paragraph, of a speech, of a chapter even a book. The précis should contain the sum and substance of the passage without leaving any important idea but without giving details. Ability to write a good précis means the ability to select the essential elements of passage and reject what is unimportant.

Qualities of a good Precis: A good précis should have the following qualities.

1. It should contain all the important ideas of the given passage.
2. It should be concise.
3. It should be well-connected and should not appear disjointed collection of sentences.
4. It should be lucid without any ambiguity.
5. It should avoid illustrations that appear to be unnecessary.

Procedure : Precis-writing is an art which requires constant practice. It has the following stages:

1. *Reading and Understanding:* The students should read the passage carefully in order to understand the contents. Repeated reading is helpful to understand the subject-matter.
2. *Noting the main points:* The leading ideas of the passage should be carefully noted by underlining the significant points.
3. *Arrangement of ideas:* The third stage consists of arranging the ideas in such a way as would make the précis appear like a connected whole.
4. *One paragraph:* It should not be written in more than one paragraph. Make the language as much your own as possible. Normally, it should be one-third the length of the given passage. But a difficult passage cannot always be summarised in about one-third its length. So, no hard and fast rule can be laid down about its length; but efforts should be made to remain brief.

Importance of Free Composition

(i) It helps student at the higher stage of learning, and in their later life.

(ii) It paves the way for logical thinking and creative work.

(iii) It develops translation ability, because pupils first think in the mother-tongue, and then translate the ideas into English.

Suggestions for improving teaching composition: A teacher can teach composition more efficiently, if he follows the following suggestions:

(i) First of all students should be prepared or motivated for composition writing. In this regard, P. Gurrey has suggested following points : (a) oral questioning, (b) using picture, (c) reading aloud, (d) short speeches, and lectures, and (e) silent reading.

(ii) The teacher should provide many good, and relevant ideas. P. Gurrey has suggested the following devices for it:

(a) Energetic questioning focussed on well-known details.

(b) Reading aloud to pupils from interesting books.

(c) Encouraging pupils to collect information in various ways.

(d) Acting, play-making and puppet-plays.

(e) Encouraging pupils to read more.

(f) Having general knowledge period once a week.

(g) Having occasional talks on interesting topics.

(h) The teacher must remove the grammatical weaknesses of pupils.

(i) The teacher must emphasise on clarity of ideas. This he can do, in the words of P. Gurrey, as follows:

"The class can be shown on the board examples of short explanations and pupils called on to find where ideas are muddled or too vague; and then asked for alternations, and finally the class can be asked to choose the clearest of these. The class can be practiced in finding unclear expression in their own writings, and in making suggestions for improvement. The teacher can question the class more precisely than usual whenever they are to write on complicated or confusing subject".

The subject of composition should be chosen by using the principles of 'utility' and 'interest'. It should be from their everyday life. According to P. Gurrey, "Indeed, it should be an unwritten law among us that pupils, who are learning a foreign language must never write about things, they have not seen in their lives – at least not until they can use the language freely and correctly in speech and writing".

Correction of Composition

The aim of correction work is to point out the mistakes of the pupils, so as to enable them to acquire the correct forms. The teacher's job is not only to find out errors but also to offer suggestion to each student as to how he can improve his composition. Teacher is expected to point out not only the mistakes of language, but also short-comings in the subject matter as also in the way of its presentation.

How to reduce mistakes?

It can be done in the following ways:

(i) Drill Work There should be plenty of drill work in the class. Such a practice in oral work helps the students in avoiding mistakes in construction of sentences.

(ii) To deal Assignments Orally : Teacher should first deal with every assignment orally. It is useful because in oral correction there is no time lag between the committing of an error, and its correction. Oral correction is done in presence of pupil and so he is made aware of his mistake.

(iii) List of Mistakes : The teacher should prepare a list of common errors and correct forms of these be given to the students.

(iv) Level or Standard of Students : The teacher must not set an exercise which is above the neonatal level or standard of the students. In the beginning controlled composition be done and only afterwards stories and essay etc., be taken up.

How to Correct Mistakes?

Following methods are used for correction work:

(i) Self-correction : The pupil should be asked to point out his own mistakes, and let the pupils correct them. In this way, the students will cultivate the habit of self-correction.

(ii) Corrections to be made in Notebooks : While making corrections in notebooks teacher may use symbolic language. He may use following symbols for various types of mistakes.

S - Spelling mistake

P - Punctuation mistake

T - Tense mistake

A - Article mistake

W - Wrong word

G - Grammar

O - Omission

? - Truth of statement questioned

! - Exaggeration

Z - Irrelevant

In most cases, mere indication of error is enough for correction. The pupils may be asked to write common mistakes in their note-books under classified heads such as (i) Errors of spelling, (ii) Errors of grammar, (iii) Errors of idioms, etc.

XV. Communication

a. Meaning of Communication : The term communication has been derived from the Latin verb *communicare.* Communicare means the 'sharing of ideas and feelings in a mood of mutuality'. Communication involves interaction, which encourages give and take. Through communication, people share knowledge, information and experience and thus understand, persuade, convert, or control their fellows.

John Dewey states, "Communication is a process of sharing experience till it becomes a common possession. It modifies the disposition of both the parties, who partake in it".

According to Edgar Dale, the implications of communication are as follows:

1. It emphasises our need to build common understanding or consensus.
2. It suggests that communication involves interaction - the give-and-take that provides feed back to persons involved in exchanging ideas.
3. It assumes a democratic philosophy of life, the dignity and respect of all, who enter into communication and the absence of manipulation of others.
4. It assumes freedom to learn and to criticise.

5. It makes central the idea of getting into the other fellow's self (empathy) and having the courtesy and sometimes the courage to let him to yours.

b. Information Communication System - Components : The essential elements of a communication system are Communicator, Message, Language, Medium, and Recipient. These elements are shown in the figures given in the following pages.

Communicator : Communicator is one who has generated an information or message. It may be an author, teacher or a scientist. He has a natural urge to share this information with his peers in the field or fellow-workers for getting their evaluation of his work.

Message : Message is what the communicator wants to convey. It should be nascent, verifiable and in standard form.

Language : It is the language in which message or information is presented. It is the vehicle to convey message. The language should be used in such a way that the users clearly and easily understand the message. Clear and simple language using precise and standard terminology will be helpful in information communication.

Medium : Medium is the mode or form through which the message or information is communicated. It can be either oral or in recorded form or in the form of audio-visual presentation. Communication through conversation or at a meeting or conference is oral in form. The recorded form of communication is through books, periodicals, reports, dissertations, theses, patents, standards, microforms, computer-readable tapes, etc. The audio-visual media constitute gramophone records, slide projections, overhead projections, video-cassettes, etc.

Recipient : A receiver can be a scientist, a technologist, a policy-maker, a teacher, a student or anybody, who makes use of the information to serve his needs.

The information in the form of message is generated by a communicator and with the help of language and some medium it is communicated to the receiver for his use. The language and the medium serve as the links so convey message from the communicator to the receiver. The smooth working of the communication system is dependent on the efficiency of these components.

(c) Communication Cycle : Effective communication is a two-way process including feedback interaction. So, it forms a communication cycle. The 'sender' formulates, encode and transmit the message through a medium to the 'receiver'. After receiving the message the 'receiver' formulate the replay message, and after encoding transmit it to the 'sender' through a medium. In some conversations, the role of the sender and the receiver will interchange. That means sender become receiver and *vise versa.*

In communication cycle, all of the communication system components are arranged in a cyclic manner. A classroom with effective communication can be cited as a typical example for a communication cycle. Effective communication is a two-way process.

(d) Channels of Communication : The channels of communication are of two types - informal and formal. The distinction between these two is simple. Informal channels are usually used when the work is in progress; formal channels are used after the work has been completed.

(e) Agencies Promoting Communication of Information : Important agencies that promote communication of information are:

(1) Authors, (2) Libraries and Information Centres, (3) Universities, (4) Governments, (5) Learned Autonomous Bodies, (6) Industrial House, Manufacturers and Traders), Mass Media like Press, Radio, Television and Motion Pictures, and (8) Book Trades.

1. Authors : Here matter is missing, please cheack it.?????????

2. Libraries and Information Centres : Distribution of information is the primary aim of a library or an information centre. To achieve this, it locates the information-bearing documents, procures them, and organises them for use. A library makes both extensive and intensive efforts to inform the users what information is available in what documents through its various bibliographical and documentation services, such as Current Awareness Service (CAS), Selective Dissemination of Information (SDI) Service, Indexing Service, Abstracting Service, etc. A library also facilitates the use of information by providing reprographic facilities and translation services. Now, Internet facility is also available in libraries.

3. Universities : The four important functions of a modern university are teaching, research, extension and publication. All these four activities are concerned with the distribution or dissemination of knowledge and with communication of information. A university is a costly apparatus. It is established by the society and is maintained by it with public money. It is necessary that the programmes and activities of the university are related to the social, economic, political, cultural and psychological realities of the society which finances it. It is to exist for the use and benefit of the society.

4. Governments : Information contained in the government publications is usually authentic, reliable, and up-to-date. Communication of information by the Government is a continuous' process intended to keep its people educated and well-informed about its policies and' programmes. The mass media, usually under the control of the government, also communicate similar information extensively.

5. Learned Societies and Autonomous Bodies : There are a large number of learned societies, "autonomous and non-autonomous" bodies —- most of them supported by the government - which are engaged in the war of research, production, commerce and service. Periodical meetings and conference of these bodies provide a good opportunity to the scientists and researchers to share their views and communicate information in an informal way. The learned periodic brought out by these bodies usually contain papers of high quality, bringing out new discoveries in the subject field they cover. Because of the respectability these journals enjoy, they are able to attract wide relationship.

6. Industrial Houses, Manufactures and Traders : Industrial houses maintain research and development units to generate technology continuously for the improvement of their products, to keep the cost of production within limits, and to bring about innovations. Besides technical reports and other literature, house journals are also brought out to communicate information of a popular nature. Industries and manufacturers circulate their literature extensively to disseminate accurate, precise and sometimes illustrated information about their products. This literature is circulated among the prospective or potential buyers free of cost.

7. Mass Media : The press, the radio, the television, the motion pictures, etc., represent major mass media which communicate both knowledge and current information to people. Through mass media, information pertaining to actual events, policies and programmes of the government in terms of the national needs and goals anticipated are communicated. Their coverage is extensive because they reach even the remote corners of the country. It is through mass communication that one becomes aware of many aspects of human life, which generally are not a part of personal experience of the recipients of the message. In view of the importance of mass media in educating, informing and inspiring the masses, the UNESCO takes special interest in mass communication, and strives to improve its technical media as well as to reduce obstacles to the free flow of information. UNESCO also supplies materials to the press, films and radio with a view to advance international understanding.

8. Book Trades : The producers of reading material and its distributors play an important role in the communication of information. The ideas of the authors are given concrete shape in the form of books, treatises, monographs, periodicals, reviews, etc., mainly through their efforts. Their main motive is profit-making. This indirectly ensures better and wider communication of the thought-provoking contents of the publications. A considerable improvement in paper technology and new developments in printing techniques have tremendously enhanced the supply of books and other forms of literature.

(f) Barriers in Information Communication : Communication of information is a two-way process. Thus, the barriers in information communication can be of two types: those encountered by the communicator, and those encountered by the recipient in accessing information.

Barriers encountered by the communicator

1. *Attitude of the person receiving information:* In an ordinary classroom the participants will be different in nature. They have differences in their familial and social background, experience, previous knowledge, I-Q level, attitude towards the topic, etc. It is one of the barriers that affect the communicator.

2. *Language unintelligible to the recipient:* This is a barrier related to the language of communication. For instance, there may be rich learning material with the communicator (teacher) to assist him. But, the language used in the material may not be easy for the learner to understand. Thus, inappropriate language will affect the communication adversely.

3. *Noise in communication:* Noise means any sort of distraction

from the surrounding that might adversely affect communication can affect communication in different ways. For example, the noise of a thunder can spoil the quality of radio or TV lessons. Classroom communication may be affected by noise from other classes, noises outside the school compound, etc.

4. *Heavy cost of communication channels:* Learning materials and modern educational strategies play a very significant role in today's teaching-learning process. It has been proved that multimedia representations and online-interactive learnings can make the learning process lively and effective. Multimedia representations give auditory as well as visual/graphical effects to the learner. Interactive learning provides skills to handle new problematic situations. But, their implementation is costly, and thus it becomes a barrier for effective communication.

Barriers encountered by the communicator

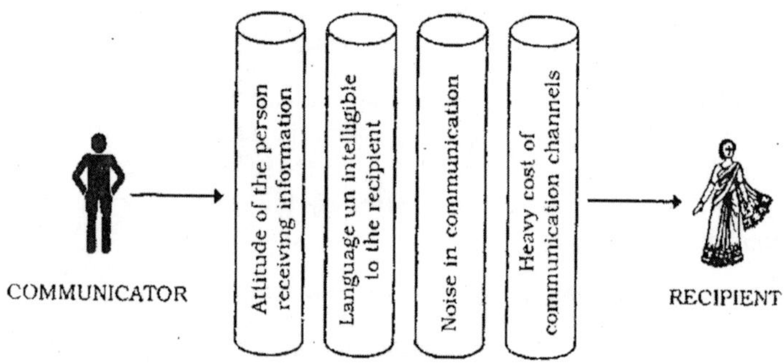

Barriers encountered by the recipient

1. *Size of the recorded knowledge:* When size of the recorded knowledge is very vast and, hence, difficult to assimilate that will become a barrier to the recipient. This suggests that the teacher should arrange the content size according to the pupils' age and capability to receive the content area within a given lapse of time.

2. *Continuous heavy flow:* Leisure is essential to reduce fatigue for all humans—-Continuous heavy flow makes the individual fatigued, and that reduces the quantity of the message communicated.

3. *Language other than the mother tongue:* The languages other than the mother tongue are very likely to create problems to recipients. A mediator is needed to overcome this problem. In classroom context, the teacher can act as a mediator.
4. *Lack of adequate knowledge of the topic:* Classroom communication is cumulative and continuous in nature. The lack of previous knowledge of the recipient will affect classroom communication. The teacher should take necessary steps to avoid this barrier according to the nature, and standard of his class. '*Vijayabheri*' conducted in some districts in Kerala is an example. *Vijayabheri* helps the students with lack of adequate previous knowledge to relearn the topics they studied earlier, during extra-classroom hours.
5. *Financial constraints:* Financial constraints make it difficult for individuals as well as institutions to procure the required instruments or media to be used to receive the information.

Barriers Encountered by the Recipient

g. Sources of Information

Before the Invention of Paper and Printing

1. Stone and Clay

From the earliest time, man has tried to preserve his thoughts for the coming generations. To begin with stone was used for this purpose. Samples of Egyptian Pictographic writing, known as *hieroglyphics,* were found in building stones dating back to 3,000 or 4,000 BC. Since writing on stone was arduous, it was gradually replaced by clay. During the Sumerian-Babylonian-Assyrian civilisations, clay was used extensively for recording information. Writing on wet clay was done by a stylus then it was baked for permanence. This writing is known as *cuneiform.* Preparation of useful clay tablets required much time, and their transportation also was difficult. Consequently, these were replaced by *papyrus,* a comparatively better communication medium.

2. Papyrus

Papyrus was made from the stem of a plant growing in the delta of the Nile River. Its stem was cut into strips which were further cut into sections. Two such sections were laid across each other with their fibre running at right angles. The fibres were immersed in water, laminated and then dried in the sun. The sheet was given a high polish. The writing on these sheets was done with a pigment. The pieces of *papyrus* were pasted together in one long strip, and rolled into a volume. Sheets were also folded and stitched together with a binding cord. It was known as a codex.

3. Silk and Skin

The supply of *papyrus plant* was limited as it could be grown in certain geographical areas only. In the third century B.C., the Chinese started using cloth as material to write upon. Camel hair brush was used for writing purposes. Since cloth was too costly to be spared for writing, *parchment* and *vellum* replaced *papyrus* as the recording medium. *Parchment* or *vellum* is not leather as it is not tanned. They are prepared with lime which gives them smoother surface.

4. Leaf and Bark of Trees

In South India, the leaf of the *palmyra palm tree* was used for writing purposes. In North India, the inner bark of the *brich tree* was used for this purpose. Amatl was the writing material used by the Mayas and Aztecs of America. Wooden strips were used by the Chinese, for writing.

5. After the invention of Paper and Printing

Before the advent of paper, information was communicated through the medial discribed above. Paper was invented in 105 A.D. by Ts'ai Lun. Since writing on the wooden strips were difficult, and the use of cloth was expensive, some other material had to be found out. The invention of paper resulted in the production and use of a wonderful writing material. The art of paper-making spread to Japan in 610, Egypt in 850, Spain in 1150, Italy in 1270, France in 1348, India in 1420, Russia in 1576-J and to the United States in 1690 A.D.

1. Gutenberg Printing

In 1440 A.D. Gutenberg invented printing from moveable type. This and that renaissance led to the increased demand for paper and consequently there was a steady growth of its production.

"The combination of paper and the printing press has probably done more to preserve man's accomplishments than any other single human achievement. Without doubt it is largely responsible for the mountain of recorded information available today." In brief, paper and printing together have joined hands to the making and preservation of documents, which act as the source of all information.

2. Document - The custodian of knowledge

Knowledge is an abstract entity. Until or unless it is embodied in some physical carrier, it cannot easily be handled, preserved and disseminated. Though the nature and physical shape of knowledge carriers have changed with the technological advances of society, documents have remained as the major means to record, preserve and disseminate knowledge. This has been true since the invention of the alphabet, and more so since the discovery of portable writing surfaces.

Information is power, and it is contained in documents in the form of kinetic power. The documents contain the wisdom of sages, experiences of philosophers and the discoveries of scientists. They are the source of all information. Further progress and development is possible only when information contained in documents is used extensively but judiciously. In view of the importance of documents, it is worthwhile to know more about them and the information they yield.

(I) Document

A document is an embodied thought. It is the record of work stored on paper or other material for easy physical handling, transportation across space and preservation through time. The thought-content of a document represents the information it carries. A document is an object that provides information. It is rather a source of information. It is the material carrier of knowledge and the stored memory of mankind. A book is a document. A thesis, a report, a pamphlet, a patent, etc., are all documents.

It may be possible to obtain information from other sources - by asking an individual or an organisation, or by attending a meeting, or by visiting an exhibition, or by listening to a radio or television broadcast; but even these sources have for the most part, gather their information from documents.

Most of the documents have been created by direct human intervention, but a few of them are directly recorded in some form through instruments. Ranganathan calls the latter as *meta-documents*. The documents which embody macro-thought are:

Own as *macro-documents* and those embodying micro-thought are called *micro-documents*. A book is a macro-document whereas an article from a journal is a micro-document.

Classification of Documents

Documents of various types have been classified into four classes by S. Ranganathan . This has been done on the basis of their physical characteristics and usage. C.W. Hanson and Denis Grogan, on the other hand, have categorised these documents into two and three categories respectively on the basis of information and characteristics.

1. Classification by Ranganathan

The following is the schematic representation of the classification of documents as given by Ranganathan:

Documents

Conventional Neo-conventional, Non-conventional, Meta-documents -

According to Ranganathan, *Conventional documents* are those which are usually recorded on paper in a natural language by writing, typing, printing or some near-printing process. These are the most popular documents in use. They include books, periodicals, maps, atlases, etc. *Neo-conventional documents* form a new class of micro-documents, such as standards, specifications, patents, data, etc. *Non-conventional documents* are those recorded in non-conventional size, shape or material. Audios, visuals, audio-visuals, microforms, etc., are included in this category, *Meta-documents* are records of phenomena made directly, unmediated by human mind. It is an instrument, record of natural or social phenomena made possible by instrument technology, for example, photography, radar, etc.

The classification of Ranganathan groups, the documents in the chronological order of their development and does not take into consideration, the information characteristics of a document. He does not make any difference between an ordinary periodical, and an indexing periodical. According to him even a book and a periodical belong to the same category, viz., conventional documents.

2. Classification by Hanson and Grogan

The schemes of classification advocated by Hanson and Grogan are mainly based on the information characteristics of documents. Hanson divides the documents into two categories - primary and secondary. Grogan goes further and divides into three categories as primary, secondary and tertiary. Brief descriptions about these are given below:

(i) Primary document : These documents represent new knowledge or new interpretation of old knowledge. They are the first published records of original research and development. Often document may be the only source of information in existence. According to Hans, the books, journals, reports, patents, theses, trade literature, standards, etc., are the main sources of primary documents. Grogan adds conference proceedings and official publication to this category, but excludes books from them.

(ii) Secondary documents : The secondary documents do not carry new and original information but guide users to the primary documents. They are compiled from the primary documents. Because, they organise primary literature in a convenient form. These documents are of three types: (a) those which selected index portions of primary literature, and help the users in finding what has been published on a given subject, such as indexes, bibliographies, and abstracts, etc., (b) those which survey selected portions of the primary literature to help the users in knowing status of given subject, such as reviews, treatises, etc., and (c) those documents which themselves contain the desired information collected and selected from primary documents. Items of information such as biographies, facts, formulas, histories, procedures, theories, etc., are derived from the primary documents and are arranged systematically in some convenient order in such secondary documents. Dictionaries, encyclopaedias, hand books, manual, etc., are some of the documents of this type.

(iii) Tertiary documents : The tertiary documents list the secondary documents. Their function is to help the researchers in retrieving the secondary sources. Directories, year books, bibliographies of bibliographies, lists of research projects in progress, guides to literature, guides to organisations, guides to libraries, textbooks, etc., are included in this category of documents.

(h) Sharing of Information Resources : No information system whether local or regional or national should exist in isolation. Arrangement for co-operation and sharing of resources should exist among the information systems on inter-country or global basis. The organisation of the National Information System in Science and Technology (NISSAT) of India is a step towards this direction. At international level, the Agricultural Science and Technology Information System (AGRIS), and the Development Science Information System (DEVSIS) are two significant examples of mutual co-operation yielding immense benefit to participants in their information communication programmes.

For sharing world information resources, the provision of on-line facilities is needed. Efforts are, however, being made for establishing a national on-line network. NICNET, the network of the National Informatics Centre, and INDONET, the network of the CMC Limited, and the Department of Electronics are being planned with this objective in view. The latter primary aims at providing integrated data communication and distributed data processing facility to all Indian users. When these two networks and some other 'chronologies like Internet become fully operational, the sharing of world information' sources will become a possibility for the Indian users spread all over the country.

Instructional Context

Definitions and Concept

"Sharing of ideas, and feelings in the mode of mutuality".

— **Dale**

"Communication is a transmission and interchange of facts, ideas, feelings or course of action".

— Leland Brown

"Communication is an exchange of facts, ideas, opinions or emotion by two or more persons. Communication is also defined as intercourse by words, letters, symbols or message, and as a way that one organisation member shares meaning and understanding with another".

—Newman and Summer

Purpose

Influencing Function

A complete communication process is necessary in influencing others or being influenced. Motivational forces are an individual are to be provided and then stimulated.

Teaching function

All teaching involves communication. Effective teaching needs effective communication.

Informing function

Communication is to inform the individual or group about the subject or concept. Becoming informed or informing others is the main purpose of communication.

Evaluation function

Evaluating one's own inputs or another's outputs or some ideological scheme demands an adequate and effective communication process.

Directing function

Directing others or being directed or instructed cannot take place without complete communication process. An order may be command order, request order or implied order.

Communication is a purposeful process.

Communication involves interaction.

Communication occurs everywhere intentionally or unintentionally.

Communication occurs at different level.

Communication is continuous.

Types of Communication

Communication has content aspect and relational aspect.

Communication is both digital (verbal) and analog (non-verbal).

Communication interchanges are based upon symmetry and/or complementarily.

Communication always takes place within a context.

Context in communication has four dimensions which includes physical, social, psychological and temporal.

Verbal communication

Verbal communication may be written, oral, inter-personal, intra-personal or public communication.

Oral communication

Oral communication may be through face-to-face interchange of over telephone, etc., its main advantage is that it provides feedback and creates a personal touch among the persons, it helps in making communication more effective as questions can be asked and answered and doubts, fears and apprehensions can be expressed and removed consequently, it promotes better understanding of ideas and intensions.

Written communication

In written communication, words are the most important means of communication. Words are not only used in express thoughts and ideas, but also attitudes, feelings and emotions towards people, objects and events. Written communication refers to messages which are expressed on paper through words or pictures, such as graph, diagrams, models, blueprints, etc., there are disadvantages of written communication, such as it does not provide the benefits of immediate feedback which face-to-face communication provides, also it tends to be expensive and time-consuming.

Inter-personal communication

Inter-personal communication means communication between at least few people, who interacts generally face to face, e.g., a telephone conversation, interview, talking to friends in a café, etc. There is emphasis on speech and non-verbal forms of communication as well.

Intra-personal communication

Intra-personal communication refers to communication with oneself. The communication is within the self and to the self e.g., thinking, working out a problem, writing diaries, hearing oneself speak. Consciously or unconsciously, intra-personal communication continues as long as a person is alive.

Non-verbal communication

Non-verbal communication is broadly defined as the area of study which includes all essentially non-linguistic phenomena which impinge on and influence the process of human interaction. Accordingly, physical structures, facial expressions, body postures, conversational silence, and human adornments such as clothing, influence communication (Smith, 1987).

Public communication

Public communication takes place in situation, where many people receive message largely from one source. A movie, television show, sermon, political speech, advertiser's message, religious leader's lecture and committee report are all example of public communication. Mass communication is public communication, because it is not directly to any given individual or group and which is transmitted electronically or mechanically, television, radio, movies, newspaper, books and magazine are all example of mass communication.

Facets of non-verbal communication

There are various facets of non-verbal communication.

Environmental factors

The physical attributes of settings affect communication, for instance, school size and design, building plan of school, illumination, furniture, temperature and abundance of colour.

Proxemics

This means the use and perception of social and personal space in the class room, that is, class room seating arrangement, teacher and student proximity, teacher use of space and organisation of bookshelves, furniture and equipment in the classroom affects the communication process.

Kinesics

Communication is also influenced by gestures, body movement, posture, and eye and facial behaviour. Major components of kinesics involve the use of gestures and postures, gaze and smile.

Sensory communication

The five sense of touch, taste, smell, sight and hearing play an important part in communication.

Para-language

The non-verbal characteristics accompanying speech such as voice pitch, volume, tempo and intensity, intruding sounds and silent pauses influence communication.

Physical Characteristics

Physical characteristics of the teacher and student influence the process of communication. It includes varying physiques, degree of attractiveness, body odour and hair or skin colour.

Artifacts

These include the adornments of human beings such as clothes, jewellery and assorted beauty aids.

Chronemics

The use of time in the classroom influences communication between the teacher the student.

Communication is a process of exchange of ideas, facts, opinions and the manner by which the receiver of message shares meaning and understanding with another. It is whole sequence of transmission and inter-change of facts, ideas, feelings, etc., process is a course of action. Communication as an organisational process affects all. It enables us to transfer information from one person to another. The ultimate object is that information transferred must be understandable to the receiver.

Elements of Communication Process

1. Message,
2. Sender,
3. Encoding,
4. Channel,
5. Receiver,
6. Decoding,
7. Acting, and
8. Feedback.

Message

It means a piece of information spoken or written to be passed from one person to another. It is the subject matter of communication; it may involve any facts, ideas, opinion, figure, feeling, attitude, or course of action including information. It exists in the mind of the communicator.

Sender

He is the sender of message or communicator or spreader, a person who transit message. In case of mechanical devices used for communication transmitter is an operator, who transmits message. The person who conveys message is known as communicator or sender. There is always a communicator in the process. He conceives and initiates message. He is a driving force to change the behaviour of the receiver.

Encoding

The process of conversion of the subject matter into symbols is called as 'encoding'. The message or subject matter or any communication is always an abstract and intangible. Transmission of the message requires the use of certain symbols. The communication or information plans and organises his ideas, facts, feelings, opinions into symbols, signs words actions, pictures and audio-visuals, etc.

Channel

The transmitter has to select the channel for sending the information. Communication channel means the medium or media through which message passes. The words, symbols, or signs selected should be transmitted to the receiver or listener through certain channel or medium. Media is plural and represents vehicles to transmit message. The communicator has to decide how best he can pass message, what he has to convey.

Receiver

There is always a receiver in the process of communication. Receiver is the person to whom the message is meant for the sender. A person, who receives the message is called receiver. Effective communication process is not complete without the existence of receiver of the message. Responding or acting to the message is done by the receiver only. It is the receiver, who receives and tries to interpret, perceive, understand and act upon the message.

Decoding

Decoding is the process of translation of an encoded message into ordinary understandable language. Receiver coverts the symbols, words or signs received from the sender to get the meaning of the message.

Acting

According to the understanding of the message the receiver acts or implements the message.

Feedback

The exchange to be complete, the information must go back to the communicator. So, that he can know the reaction of the receiver. The sending back of the knowledge about the message to the transmitter is known as feedback. It ensures that the receiver has received the message and understood in the same sense as the sender meant. Feedback enables the communicator to carry out corrections or amendments or change message to be effective. **Dyadic Communication**

Communication requires participants and purposes. A one-to-one interaction between persons is a usual form of speech communication. The interaction between two persons is generally referred to as 'dyadic communication'. Here the reactions of the sender and receiver are mutually observable. According to these reactions the participants frequently change their roles. Dyadic communication includes face-to-face conversation, telephonic conversation, interview, etc.

(a) Face to face conversation (dialogue)

Conversation or dialogue is an oral communication between two persons. A dialogue is usually an informal or friendly exchange of ideas. We can say anything we like to anyone at any time but we do not do so. There are many social constraints, and we should be aware of these to communicate effectively.

Formal and informal instruction

The varied experiences together with formal and informal instruction will build awareness about the theme involved. Conversation is a natural process and teachers should practise it in a natural way in the class room. A number of situations should be created in which students can continuously and constantly practise conversing.

Points to consider during conversation

It is good to analyse your habits while conversing. You should be on the lookout for the following points for self-analysis.

1. Whether you can easily find a topic for conversation.
2. Whether you have proper fluency.

3. Whether you are a good listener or whether you are not giving a chance for others to speak.
4. Whether you are criticising others often.
5. Whether you have awkward mannerisms.
6. Whether you respect others' point of view.

Hints for improving conversation skills

1. The topic of conversation should be of interest to both the participants; otherwise, it will become a monologue.
2. Respect others' point of view. Do not criticise others or go on disagreeing their point of view all the time.
3. Speak in clear and simple language. Avoid superfluous and bombastic words and phrases. This will hamper the smooth flow of conversation.
4. Radiate charm and cheerfulness. This will show that you are interested in the conversation.
5. Keeping eye contact, use of proper body language, etc., are necessary requirements for keeping the conversation alive. Standing too close to a person or looking away while speaking may be equally disturbing.
6. Don't monopolise the conversation; give the other person a chance to speak.

How to write a dialogue

To write a dialogue successfully, the writer has to first put himself in the position of the two peoples expressing their opinions in a natural situation. A written dialogue should appear natural. First step for writing a dialogue is to make an outline of the dialogue in advance.

Steps

1. The situation in which the participants engage themselves in the dialogue should be carefully thought of. The opinion or points of view about the points which might be expressed should be jotted down.
2. Arrange these arguments or ideas in a logically sequential order. Try to reflect over how people talk in a real situation.

3. Apply imagination and creativity in shaping the dialogue. Develop a clear idea of the nature of the imaginary persons taking part in the conversation. Make the dialogue appropriate to the nature of their thinking and speaking. For example, a studious and bookish person will talk differently from an outgoing athlete.
4. The final form of the dialogue should depict a natural conversation. Take care to avoid bookish phrases.

Hints

1. Begin the conversation in an interesting way. In the same manner, the conclusion also should be appropriate.
2. Give the two participants in the conversation equal chance to express themselves. Don't let the dialogue turn into a monologue.
3. The conversation should appear spontaneous and natural. It should be as far as possible similar to a conversation in real life. Here, often speakers counter question each other, sometimes there may be an abrupt ending.
4. For example., A: "What will you do if he threatens to fire you? B: "Well, what would you do?" Exclamation, interjection, etc., should be used when the situation so demands. But care should be taken not to overdo the same.
5. Even though the language should be realistic in nature, care should be taken not to use crude or slang language.

XVI. Language Skills

- Listening,
- Speaking,
- Reading, and
- Writing.

Listening

It is generally considered a passive skill whereas speaking is considered an active skill. However, listening is not totally passive, and it is also an active skill because it involves decoding a message and understanding it. Moreover, the listener has also to indicate by his response, if he has/or has not understood the message.

The skill of listening can be developed through systematic teaching. To cultivate listening ability it is desirable to give a good practice in listening-extensive and intensive. Extensive listening implies exposures to a wide variety of structures and sounds. Intensive listening is concerned with just one or two specific points.

Listening Skills

- Listening is found to be most effective when it is done in preparation for speaking. Indian students generally suffer from the following weaknesses which hamper their ability inadequate phrases that are understood.
- Inability to maintain attention.
- Inability to understand pronunciation other than the personal or regional pronunciation.
- Inability to understand fast speech.
- Inability to understand against background noise through acoustic/ electrical interference.

Following remedial measures may be adopted

- For this the students should enrich their vocabulary.
- Dictation helps in sharpening attention. Listening to broadcasts or recordings or films also help in it.
- The student should learn correct pronunciation for each word.
- For the removal of this the teacher can adjust his speech and clarify to the capacity of the class and then gradually speech up.
- For it to the tackled seriously, we need specially prepared recordings and tape recorders are therefore indispensable.
- Apart from these activities, the students should be trained in listening to connected speech at normal conversational speed. For such listening

- Practice, records and pre-recorded cassettes can be used, or the teacher himself can speak, the passage at normal conversational speed.

Speaking Skill

It is already been emphasised that practice in listening should precede practice in speaking.

The practice in speaking may be started by the teacher with dialogues. For such a practice, dialogues on simple, contextualised situations may be tried between pair of students. In this way, the teacher should play the role of a guide and must not curb the freedom of expression. In this way, enough opportunities are provided to the students to practice certain phonological, grammatical and lexical items.

Another technique that can be used is reading aloud, however this technique is objectional on both psychological and pedagogical grounds as it provides practice only to a few students and bores everybody else.

Some other objectives to it are as follows:

- It can be embracing to the reader is so far as it tends to make himself-conscious.
- It interferes with the proper business of the reading of the lesson, i.e., to increase the reading speed.
- The practice is random and non-specific.
- The material chosen from the book is generally not connected with situation.

While giving a practice in oral English, the following points to be given due consideration:

- Teacher should write down the correct transcription for any mispronunciation that he hears.
- Teacher should pay particular attention to the following:
  (a) Misplaced stress on syllables and words or absence of stress at all.

(b) Confusion between sounds with meaningful contrasts.

(c) Failure to discriminate between long and short-diphthongs.

(d) Interference of the phonological system of the mother tongue of the learner.

(a) Failure to aspirate initial / p /,/t/and /k/.

(b) A tendency to aspirate /h/ when not required.

(c) Production of the harsh sounds /r/ in words likes 'wonderful', 'far' etc.

(d) Misapplication of lexis and idioms.

For the development of the skill of speaking English in his students, it is desirable for an English teacher to speak English correctly, and he should ensure that his own spoken English is good.

Teaching Speaking Skills

The skills of listening, reading, and writing without paying attention to speaking, some other methods emphasised speaking and ignored other skills.

- A typical communicative classroom is more than they would in a classroom that follows language learning methods such as the grammar translation method.
- Teachers must adequately deal with all the four language skills.
- The speaking skills of students are generally ignored.
- The prevailing test/examination pattern is an ease in point.
- Students take today require then to write the answers.
- Students' oral skills in the target language are only occasionally assessed.
- Make to difficult to work on students speaking skills in any meaningful way.
- Students are reluctant to speak in the target language because of fear.
- Teachers feel inadequate to speak in the foreign language during classes.

- Teacher must begin to work on their students speaking skills from the beginning of instruction.
- The sound patterns of the new language are different from the sound patterns of the students' native language.
- Early attention to pronunciation is, therefore, beneficial to students.
- Teacher for use in developing the speaking skills of students.
- Teacher can make use of information gap exercises and presentations of dialogues.
- Students speaking skills improve where they listen to or hear the target language as often as possible.
- Speaking and listening skills, therefore, support each other in that practice in one skill helps to improve the development of the other.

Spoken English is difficult, but important. It is difficult because,

- Spelling offers or clue to pronunciation.
- Twenty six letters do the work of forty four sounds.
- The same letters stands for different sounds.
- The same sound is represented by different letters.
- Silent letters do not work.

Improving speaking skills

Techniques to improve speaking skills are similar to those used for the other language skils.

- Used for the development of speaking skills should be based on the authentic use of language.
- To involve using the target language for purposes.
- Given to the students should be within their capabilities.
- Students should be asked to speak about topics that are intensically interesting for them.

- Given to the students should be structured around a given purpose for speaking.
- Should allow students to express their own ideas and opinions and to bring aspects of themselves and their personalities into the classroom.
- This will help increase students motivation to students, and, therefore, be more beneficial to their overall language development.

Group Activity

- Small groups to discuss an issue or solve a problem.
- Interacting with other person.
- Teacher should expect the speech of their students to be less grammatical than their written work.

Suggestion

- No confusion in the pronunciation of the words spoken.
- To practice the oral drill like individual, group chorus and repetition drills.
- A new sound word is introduced the teacher should use number of words having the same sound and same syllable.

Reading Skill

Like listening it is a decoding process. But it is very complex process and involves many physical, intellectual and often emotional reactions. Further it entails the ability to recognise graphic symbols and their corresponding vocal sounds. Thus, reading skill consists of three important components, viz.

- Recognition of the graphic marks.
- The correlation of these with formal linguistic elements.
- The correlation of these with meaning.

Importance of Reading

Dr West after an extensive study on Indian pupils suggested that reading should be given the key place in the total scheme of teaching English as a foreign language.

Teaching of reading is important because:

- Reading indicates towards knowing of the language.
- Reading helps in knowing world's news, important information through newspapers, journals, books, etc.
    (i) It is a source of recreation. In leisure hours, one can go through books, magazines, journals, etc. C.C. Fries rightly remarks, "Our main purpose in developing the ability to read among our children is that we wish to put them in possession of the power gaining pleasure and profit from the printed pages".
    (ii) It is a good source of self-education.
    (iii) W.S. Gray says, "Reading is a form of experience. Reading brings us in contact with the minds of great authors, with the written account of their experiences, their recorded lives and the advancements made by them in various fields".

(i) According to Lord Bacon, "Reading maketh a full man".

(ii) It gives the learner a full control words and patterns which they come across during the process of speaking.

(iii) Prof Ghanchi and Trivedi remark, "in fact education of child is inperfect, unless he is equipped with the ability to read, to decipher, to interpret and to understand properly the contents of a reading material. The intellectual advancement of the child is strictly limited, if he is unable to read".

Aims of Teaching Reading

- To read English with accuracy.
- To read with correct pronunciation.
- To read with fluency.

- To read with understanding.
- To enable students to take pleasure in reading.
- To enable students to use ideas gained from reading in other situations.
- To enable pupils to form a habit of reading.
- To enable students to read material in English after school life e.g., books at university level, correspondence, reports, magazines, and newspaper, etc.
- To widen the 'eye-span' which means the number of words that our eyes in one complete movement.

Important methods of teaching reading are:

1. Alphabet method,
2. Syllabic method,
3. Word method,
4. Phrase method,
5. Sentence method,
6. Story method, and
7. Phonic method.

1. Alphabetic Method

It is also called the 'ABC method, and 'Spelling method'. It is used in West as well as in East. It was invented by Greeks and Romans and used till the end of middle ages.

Procedure

Following steps are undertaken to teach in this method:

1. Teaching the pupils in the names of the letters in their alphabetic order.
2. Repeating ABC.... XYZ until known by heart.
3. Combining two or more letters to form a word., e.g., h-e is 'he', s-h-e is 'she'

4. Combining words into phrases and sentences.
5. Reading passages. Thus, the procedure is

   Letters ® words ® phrases ® sentences.

Limitations of the Method

1. It is a difficult and lengthy method.
2. It is not pleasant.
3. It is dull and monotonous.
4. It is unpsychological method.
5. It does not expand the eye-span, and
6. It neglects conceptual and perceptual learning.

Horace Mann has observed, "I am satisfied that our greatest error in teaching children lies in beginning with the alphabet. How can one, who as yet is utterly incapable of appreciating the remote benefits which in after life reward, the acquisition of knowledge, derive any pleasure from an exercise which presents neither beauty to his eyes nor music to his ears, nor sense to his understanding.

2. Syllable method

The teaching by this method starts with the teaching of syllables. Thus, in this method is unit of teaching is syllable and not an alphabet.

Procedure

1. Syllables are used directly.
2. Syllables are combined to form words and sentences.

Limitations

1. The syllable structure of English is complex, and thus it becomes hard for pupils to read as most of them are in their tender age.
2. To remember all the syllable-structures of English puts a heavy memory load on pupils.
3. Since this method is analytic, so it is hard to understand.
4. Syllables do not carry meaning and are insignificant.

3. Word Method

In this method, a whole word is given for reading from the beginning words are presented with the help of audio-visual aids. Teacher may use the picture of 'shoe' and the word 'shoe' written under it. After showing the picture, teacher asks the students to look at it. He says 'shoe' and writes the word on the blackboard. The pupils are taught to read it at sight by associating it with the accompanying picture. This method is also known as "look and say method" and "see and say method". It is based on the following assumptions:

1. A word has its own characteristic form. It helps the eyes in recognising it.
2. The smallest language with which has a meaning is a word.
3. The basic units of thought are words.

The second step in teaching by this method is the repetition of the word many a times by the pupils. This he can do by looking at the picture, and the black-board.

Next step is to introduce sentences by joining many words.

Finally, the practice of reading is done by reading the text book.

This method is considered better than the alphabetic method. However, Thompson and Wyatt think that it is not different from alphabetic method. "It is as much the alphabetic because ultimately the recognition of a word depends upon recognition of component letters, their sequence".

Limitations

- It encourages the bad habit of reading one word at a time.
- All words cannot be taught by using pictures.
- It fails to develop the skill of deciphering new words.
- There are abstract words; full meanings cannot be got through single, separate words.
- It does not help in developing accuracy and independence in recognising words.
- Since the child's is required to remember many symbols of words

it strains his memory.

- It ignores spellings.
- It helps in developing the habit of guessing.

This method has been recommended by various scholars in spite of all these limitations of the method.

P.C. Wren, "It is the one and only rational method".

Prof Morris, "The look and say method are unquestionably the means of inculcating the reading skill, in view of the phonetic character of English orthography".

4. Phase method

It lies mid-way between word and sentence method. This method is based on the following assumptions:

- Phrases are more interesting than words.
- Phrases convey meaning.
- At each fixation of an eye, a reader recognises not a word, but a group of words.
- Phrases are more suitable units of reading.

Procedure

- The teacher prepares a list of phrases and writes one phrase on the black board.
- He asks the pupils to look at the phrase attentively.
- The teacher reads the phrase and pupils repeat it several times.
- New phrase are compared with the phrases already taught.

Advantages

- According to Palmer, the main supporter of this method, "the word is too small a unit of speech and the sentences is too long a unit to be read at a time".

- It helps in extending eye-span.
- Rapid growth in the teaching has been found.
- Phrases can be presented with more interesting material aids.

Writing Skill

Definition

Writing is of immense importance. According to Bacon, "Reading maketh a full man, conference a readying man and writing an exact man".

Emphasising the importance of writing Mahatma Gandhi says, "Fair and legible hand-writing makes a man perfect in all walks of life".

In the words of Bell, "writing is a tool used to enable us to express what is in our mind and for some people is almost as important as speech".

Teaching of Writing

According to Bell, "Writing is a difficult art: it requires complete control of the muscles of the hand and wrist and this control a small child does not neutrally possess," so there is need to teach writing. It involves the following:

- Teaching to develop the skill of controlling the small muscles of the fingers and the wrist, while writing.
- Teaching co-ordination of hand and eye.
- Getting students to do exercises in written work.

Teaching mechanics of writing

Mechanics of writing includes the following:

- Make letters of the right shape and size.
- Giving proper spacing between letters, words and lines.
- Using capital letters and other punctuation marks.
- Controlling the small muscles of the fingers and wrist to have fluent movement in writing.

Teaching writing mechanics has three stages as follows:

- Preparation for writing,
- Learning to write, and
- Mastering a mature style of hand-writing.

Learning to write

After having some practice in drawing, the child starts learning to write the letters of the alphabets. He learns small letters first and capital letters afterwards. Generally, he learns letters in graphs of four or five letters of similar shape and not in their proper order.

For this, the teacher should demonstrate the shape and form of the letters on the chalk-board.

Learning the alphabetical order

At about the end of first year, the order of letter in the alphabets can be taught as follows:

- Capital letters group one – round letter based on circles e.g., O C Q.
- Capital letters group two – letters formed by strokes; e.g., I,L,E,F etc.
- Capital leters group three – letters based on curves; e.g., B,D,P,R,S,U,Y etc.

General constructions to be kept in mind while teaching writing

Following considerations must be kept in mind while teaching writing.

(i) **Choice of Script:** The beginning should be made with print script and then change over to cursive writing.

(ii) There are two main styles of writing, (a) vertical, and (b) slanted. In vertical style, letters are written in vertical fashion (/). It is best style of writing. The slanted style is of two types:

(a) Forward slant,

(b) Backward slant.

Forward slant is better than backward slant, because the later hinder speeds. The teacher must emphasise the vertical style. The teacher should see it to that students do not write letters in more than one style. The letters necessarily should have uniform style.

(iii) Writing a material,

For teaching writing, the following materials are mainly needed:

1. Black-board and chalk,
2. Tray of sand,
3. Kinder-garden box,
4. Paper and pencil,
5. Exercise book, and
6. Flash cards.

(iv) Posture

Posture is an important consideration that has to be kept in mind while teaching writing. Students should be made to adopt good postures during writing. At their desk they should sit comfortable in erect position. Both their feet should rest on the ground. The body should lean slightly forward the hips, but should not touch the desk.

The head should be so held so that his eyes are about 13 inches away from the paper. The chest should be clear of the edge of the desk; both forearms should be within two or three inches of the elbows and should rest lightly on the desk.

Deciding qualities of a good writing

Before starting teaching, teacher must know the qualities of good hand writing. They are as follows:

1. Legibility,
2. Attractiveness,
3. Uniformity,
4. Distinctiveness,

5. Good styled,
6. Speedily, and
7. Correctly spaced.

Causes of bad hand writing

Some of the causes of bad hand writing are as follows:

- Sometimes it is due to imitation of bad examples.
- The use of ball pens or fountain-pens at very early stages of writing.
- Lack of good sitting arrangement.
- Bad sitting postures.
- Not so good quality of paper and ink,
- Ways of holding pen or pencil.
- Lack of freedom of hand movement.
- Lack of practice in writing.
- Physical defects in the students.

Measures to improve bad hand writing

Following measures are likely to help the students in acquiring good hand writing:

- Use of four-lined notebooks.
- Sitting in proper posture.
- Having the proper position of desks.
- Use of calligraphy note books.
- Arranging competitions.
- Showing model hand writing.
- Checking mistakes.

- Holding the pen properly.
- Using black boards for difficult words
- Motivating pupils to find their own mistakes.
- Use of proper writing material.
- Individual attention.
- Sympathetic treatment.
- Adequate practice.
- Arranging handwriting competitions.

For improvement of handwriting, it is desirable to give adequate exercises in writing viz., transcription, dictation and composition should be given to the students.

XVII. Supplementary Skills

- Study skills,
- Reference skills.

Study skills

Note-making is the process where in the individuals are asked to make a note of important points from reference books, newspapers, reports, etc., and then prepare a brief summary of them. The students may be encouraged to prepare summaries of long reports or to prepare a brief note from the reference books or newspapers. They should also be trained to narrate or describe a good number of events in a nutshell in short span of time. Note-making involves reading, comprehension and analysis. Sometimes people need to read a particular piece of work repeatedly in order to get a thorough understanding of this subject. Then they may be asked to give a gist of ideas contained therein. The students may be encouraged to make a note of important events from the books, reports, newspapers, etc., that they read regularly. Note-making activity will help them to sharpen their concentration and identify important information leaving the irrelevant matter. While making notes first person narration has to be re-written in the third person. Note-making activity will develop in them, the necessary study skills.

Characteristics of Note-taking/making skills

- While preparing the notes, the draft should be precise. It should include essential points.
- Ignore all irrelevant information and minor points.
- Present the text in a nutshell.
- Use abbreviations and symbols.
- Provide the essence of the whole topic.
- Help to recapitulate the whole text at a later date.
- Help to give instant comprehension for the readers.
- Process involved in note-taking / making.
- The person interested in developing note-taking kills should read the whole text, at least twice.Decide the little for the text.
- Reduce the text into an outline retaining all the salient points.
- Structure the whole text by dividing it into main and sub-pionts on the basis of the title given to the text.
- Prepare the note in such a manner that it should give scope for the writer / reader to reconstruct the original passage at a later date.
- Maintain logical sequence of ideas given in the text.

Advantages of note-taking/making individual

- To organise the thoughts in a logical and sequential order.
- To provide a quick reference of the text before one goes to give a lecture on the given topic.
- To have a gist of ideas reflected in the text.
- To revise the given text and make it suitable to the context.
- To facilitate easy recapitulation of the text.
- To reconstruct the present a large text in a concise and compact form.

- Text depending on the mode of presentation.
- To develop the skills of comprehension, analysis and presentation of a text suitable to the occasion.
- The teachers in the secondary schools should cultivate the habits of note-taking / making among their students right from the early stages, so that the students will be able to communicate their ideas effectively. They may be encouraged to practice a lot in developing these skills both in the classroom and from the surroundings.

Advantages of a dictionary

- A good dictionary provides us with spelling, phonetic transcription, syllable division and stress of a word.
- The differences between British and American spelling.
- The differentces between British and American pronunciation.
- The grammar of a word (whether a particular word is used as noun, verb, adjective and adverb).
- Different meanings associated with a word with differences in the context.
- Thus, a dictionary can be understood as one of the important reference manuals one can use in one's own walk of life. This helps an individual get a thorough command over the language.

References Skills

Language learning is basically a skill in language learning. Every child is expected to acquire mastery over some supplementary skills through reference materials. These supplementary skills are otherwise known as 'Reference skills'.

Some reference materials are:

- Dictionaries,
- Thesaurus, and
- Encyclopaedia.

Some of the techniques are followed in dictionaries:

- The alphabetical order of words.
- The guide words at the top of each page.
- The abbreviations used for different purposes in the usage.
- The key to entries at the beginning.
- The detailed guide at the end, and.
- Appendices.

Advantages

- Spelling, phonetic transcription, syllable division and stress of a word.
- The differences between British and American spelling.
- The differences between British and American pronunciation.
- The grammar of a word (whether a particular word is used as noun, verb, adjective or adverb).
- Different meanings associated with a word with differences in the context.

Dictionaries

A dictionary is a book specially designed to list out and explain the words of a language that are normally arranged in an alphabetical order. Dictionaries, which are an integral part of any learning process, are the most important of all the reference manuals.

Some dictionaries

- The Oxford Dictionary of English gives us the etymology and formation of a word.
- The Random House Dictionary of the English language gives us the synonyms and antonyms of a word.
- Dictionary by Daniel Jones which provides us the systematic pronunciation of different words in English language.

Thesaurus

Thesaurus is a book that lists words in groups of synonyms and related concepts. Rich words in the language arranged alphabetically, each with a plentiful supply of alternative and connected expressions. Selected antonyms have also been added wherever appropriate. Thesaurus contains the accurate, comprehensive and up todate picture of the English language today.

Thesaurus

Thesaurus is one of the important reference manuals, a learner can use at an advanced stage. A thesaurus is a book containing a stock of words, synonyms and antonyms. It is different from a dictionary in the sense that it does not define a word or give the meaning or usage of word. However, it follows the alphabetical order in the arrangement of words and contains abbreviations. A thesaurus helps the learner to find the related words, when he has one of the meanings of different words; it helps to increase the vocabulary of the learners. A thesaurus and a dictionary are complementary to each other. Both the manuals are used at higher levels of learning.

Features

- 3,50,000 synonyms and antonyms grouped under 15,000 headwords.
- A-Z list of headwords for easy reference.
- Synonyms grouped by register, so that the user can select the most appropriate in any context.
- Different meanings distinguished with examples and key synonyms leading the user straight to the sense required.
- Hundreds of words organised in family sets.

Advantages

A thesaurus helps the learners to

- Know the synonyms of a word.

- Know the antonyms of the words given,
- Increase their mastery over vocabulary,
- Use the language effectively while writing different articles or essays.
- Have a glance at different words with the same meaning instantly.
- Select the appropriate word suitable to the context from among those words with similar meaning.

Advantages

Encyclopaedia provide us with

- Quick reference,
- In-depth information on a given subject,
- The subject – specific information, and
- The required information instantly.

Encyclopaedia

Encyclopaedias are a kind of reference manuals wherein we come across more information on a particular topic, subject or author. These encyclopaedias run into many volumes and contain a lot of information relating to the subject concerned. The last volume is called the index volume. These encyclopaedias are known as quick reference manuals.

In most of the big libraries, we find encyclopaedias like Encyclopaedia Britannica, Encyclopaedia Americana, Columbia Encyclopaedia etc. Further, we also find certain subject-specific encyclopaedias like Encyclopaedia of Science, Encyclopaedia of Agriculture, Encyclopaedia of Education etc. Encyclopaedias cater to the needs of the advanced learners, teachers, research workers, etc. The publishers of the Encyclopaedias bring out supplements every year with a view to update the information contained therein. These supplements are known as 'yearbooks'.

XVI. Pictures for Language Learning

Listening is as much important as speaking, reading and writing. Listening is so significant that one must be skilled in how to listen, why to listen, when to listen, and to what and to whom to listen. Listening is a skill of learning in the teaching and learning process.

Either made by the teacher or brought for classroom teaching can be divided into two categories.

- Those designed primarily for classroom teaching.
- Those used primarily for decorating the classroom and giving a background that conveys a visual impression of the country.

Whether the language is spoken, both are important, but they have different uses and should be handled differently.

Pictures are the cheapest and easily available teaching aids. These can be handled judiciously to present a lot of information. Pictures, photographs, art pictures, etc., are used to present grammatical structures, vocabulary or content, sometimes pictures may mislead the students, so the teacher should be very careful in using pictures.

Verbal or written statements accompanying the pictures are shown to them. These pictures also provide the systematic cultural experience necessary for a full understanding and use of the language. Selection of pictures and the order of presentation are the two crucial aspects of using pictures to teach English in the lower classes.

Values of Pictures

- Pictures are necessary for a proper understanding of the language. They are the best aids, next to only to concrete objects themselves. They are the cheapest and most readily available.
- They assume greater importance after the introduction of English as a second language. They reduce the use of the mother-tongue in the English class for saves a lot of time.
- Pictures illustrate actions that cannot be performed in class.
- They explain much of the background of a language.
- The child is spontaneously interested in pictures and pays greater attention to and interest in the pictures and the lessons. Pictures are useful in the creation of an English atmosphere in the classroom.

- Pictures are useful in the teaching of all types of lessons informative, descriptive, narrative or reflexive. They develop taste and artistic imagination.
- But there are certain limitations of picture also. Abstract words are not picturable. There are other words and expressions beyond the scope of pictorial illustration. The importance and place of verbal explanation in English teaching cannot be reduced or underestimated English cannot be learnt through dumb shows alone.

The Use of Pictures

- Picture can be used to explain the meaning of words and expression. They can be used as illustrative material.
- They can be used at stages of the lesson, motivation, development, review and follow-up work.
- Oral and written work can be based on pictures (picture question).
- Picture dramatisation is interesting work.
- For drill and repetitive work in the prose, lesson, pictures are useful. For eliciting appreciation, teaching grammar and serialising events of a story, pictures can be used.
- But over use of pictures has its own dangers. Independent recall of the words and expression denoted by pictures is sundered difficult in some cases. If words are taught through pictures alone, the vocabulary of pupils will be narrow in range and small in the nature of words.
- Pictures should be visible to whole class. They must be hung in good light advantage position. Picture boards may be used for simultaneous display, or serial display of a set of pictures. The positions of permanent pictures may be changed seasonally and periodically for imaginery variety. New pictures may be replaced older ones. The teacher can encourage pupils own private collection of pictures relevant to the lessons.

XIX. Central Institute of Indian Languages

Central Institute of Indian Languages, Mysore a subordinate office has been helping in evolving and implementing the language policy of the government of India and co-ordinating the development of Indian languages by conducting research in the areas of language analysis, language pedagogy, language technology and language use in society, a bias towards problem solving and national integration.

Central Institute of Indian Languages has following three schemes.

Scheme I

The first scheme is for the development of Indian languages through developing man power production of materials in modern Indian Languages including tribal languages.

- Tribal and Indian border languages,
- Socio-linguistics,
- Phonetics,
- Psycho-linguistics,
- Materials production and training,
- Evaluation and testing,
- Distance education,
- Educational technology,
- Lexicography, and
- Translation.

Scheme II

The second scheme is for the implementation of three-language formula. This is done through training of teachers of the secondary schools, deputed by various states and UTs. The RLCs conduct various teachers' training programme and prepare instructional materials. The ten months intensive course in Indian languages began in July in different centres. The target of admission for this course in SRLC: 120, ERLC: 80, WRLC: 60, NRLC: 60, VTRC: each 40, total: 400.

Scheme III

The scheme provides financial assistance to individuals and voluntary organisations for publication in Indian languages (other than Hindi, Urdu, Sindhi, Sanskrit, and English) inclusive of tribal languages. The first grants-in-aid meeting were held in Mysore on 10.9.1998 which recommended purchase of 99 books and for publication assistance for eight manuscripts.

XX. Central Institute of English and Foreign Languages

In order to bring about substantial improvement in the substandards of teaching/learning of English, the government is giving assistance through the CIEFL, Hyderabad for the setting up of at least one district centre for English language in each state. Twenty-six district centres were initially sanctioned. There were 11 district centres in operation as on 31st March 1998, in different parts of our country. The government is also providing assistance to regional institutes of English language teaching institutes of different states through the CIEFL for strengthening them. There are at present two regional Institutes of English and nine English language teaching institutes. Apart from this grants also given to voluntary organisations/individuals for publication and purchase of books in English language.

XXI. Kendriya Hindi Shiksha Mandal, Agra

The Kendriya Hindi Shiksha Mandal, Agra, is an autonomous institution established by the government of India under overall control of the Ministry of Human Resource Development (Department of Education). The Mandal runs "Kendriya Hindi Sansthan" under its aegis with its headquarters at Agra and centres at Delhi, Hyderabad, Mysore, Guwahati and Shillong.

The sansthan conducts Hindi Shikshan Nishant (MED, Hindi Shikshan Parangat (B.Ed), Hindi Shikshan Praveen, four years Hindi Shikshan Diploma and Intensive Hindi teaching orientation courses. The Sansthan also runs courses for the teaching of Hindi to foreigners at Agra under the scheme of "propagation of Hindi Abroad". The Sansthan also offers in-service training to teachers.

The tribal language research unit is working on the development of the language teaching materials for Nagaland. The language technology and audio-visual unit is involved in the preparation of remedial audio-material for various linguistic areas especially for northern- eastern region.

The institute also publishes research-oriented material related with Hindi language and literature. The institute has published eight books, two journals and 66 lessons for correspondence course in the discipline of applied linguistics, language teaching and literature.

Under the scheme "*Hindi Seva Samman Yojana*", 13 eminent Hindi scholars have been selected for *Hindi Seva Samman* during the year 1998-99 for their distinguished contribution in the fields of development and propagation of Hindi, research and creative literature, scientific and technical literature in Hindi and also Hindi journalism.

XXII. Formula in Conversation

In our day-to-day conversation with people we use certain set expressions in conversation. Some of these are called 'formulas' which are group of words used regularly on certain occasions. For example, expressions of:

1. Greeting,
2. Leave taking,
3. Gratitude,
4. Regret,
5. Forms of request,
6. Asking permission,
7. Appreciation,
8. Agreeing,
9. Disagreeing, and
10. Showing surprise.

1. Greeting

The general set expressions used for greeting and responses are given below:

* How do you do? How do you do?
* How are you? Fine, thank you.
* Good Morning/Afternoon/Evening. Good Morning/Afternoon/ Evening.

2. Leave Taking

* Good bye! Good bye!

This is used in rather formal situations.

* 'Bye', 'Bye-bye', 'See you', etc. can be used between friends.
* Good night! Is an expression used while taking leave late in the evening.

3. Gratitude

* Thank you, Thanks a lot.

I'm extremely grateful to you.

I'm very grateful/obliged to you.

That was/very kind/nice/generous of you.

The response to these expressions is given below:

* You're welcome. It's my pleasure. Not at all. Don't mention it. Thank you.

4. Regret

* I am sorry. Please forgive me. Pardon me.

  I apologise.

  The expressions used for granting forgiveness are given below:

* That all right.

  It doesn't matter. Don't worry. Forget it!

5. Forms of requests

Would I repeat what you said?

Will you say that again?

Could I write that on the black board?

It is common to add 'please' with the above expressions. For example, will you say that again, please?

The responses to requests are given below:

* Certainly of course! Sure.

6. Asking permission

* Can I go to the cinema?
* Will you allow me to go to the beach?
* May I go to the office?

  Can I borrow your umbrella?
* Could I speak to Aysha, please?
* Could you permit me to read the book?

7. Appreciation

To show appreciation or regard you may use any one of the expressions given below:

* That's nice.
* Excellent!
* That's great!
* Wonderful!

8. Agreeing

* I agree with you.
* Couldn't agree more.
* That's what I think too.
* Exactly.

9. Disagreeing

* I don't agree with you.

* I disagree.
* I'm afraid I can't agree with it.
* I don't think that's right.
* Certainly not!
* Sorry, but I disagree with your point of view.

10. Showing surprise

* What a surprise!
* That's amazing!
* I don't believe it!
* What a pleasant surprise!
* How astonishing!

Dialogues to practice

Three short dialogues

(i) Hello

Shada - Hello!

Shamil - Hi Shada. How do you do? Shada - How do you do?

Shamil - Haven't seen you for a long time. Where were you?
Shada - That's exactly what I had in my mind too.

(ii) Good bye

Sam - Bye Nimil. See you on Friday.

Nimil - Good bye Sam. Have a nice day.

Sam - Thanks, same to you.

Nimil - Thanks.

(iii) Asking time

A - Excuse me. What time is it?

B - Half past three.

A - Thank you.

B - You're welcome.

Getting Introduced

Shaheen - good morning. I'am Shaheen. What's your name?

Zamil - Zamil

Shaheen - Are you a Malayalee?

Zamil - No, I'am a Tamilian. Where are you from?

Shaheen - I'm from Punjab.

Zamil - Are you a Punjabi?

Shaheen - No, I am a Bengali, but I've been brought up and educated in Punjab.

Asking Directions

A - Excuse me. Could you tell me where the post-office is?

B - Well..., Go straight, at the junction turn left. It's on the side of the road.

A - Is it far?

B - No, not really.

A - Thank you.

B - You are welcome.

At the Library

Librarian - Can I help you?

Ruby - Yes, I would like to look at books on Indian Music.

Librarian - You will find some books on music in the reference section.

Ruby - What I wan't is a book on Indian classical music.

Librarian - I'm sorry, but you know we don't stock many books on music, and art in this library.

Ruby - Could you suggest any other library?

Librarian - Well you better search the public library Ruby. Thank you, Sir. Librarian - My pleasure.

Example

Deepa and Reena are discussing their plans for the weekend.

Deepa: What are you doing this weekend, Reena?

Reena: I've not made any special plans.

Deepa: How do you like the idea of going to the cinema?

Reena: That sounds great; but don't you think I should get my parent's permission?

Deepa: I'll come to your house and meet your parents.

Reena: Hey, that's a good idea.

Deepa: Can I come in the evening?

Reena: Yes, I don't think they are going out tonight.

Deepa: Ok fine, I'll see you in the evening. Bye.

Thus a dialogue is a real and natural verbal expression and non-verbal cues like gestures, facial expressions, and eye contact are used meaningfully. Thus, there is sharing of information between people during a conversation.

Conversation and dialogue bring people together, and build up a well-knit society. Common interests and concerns can be shared which would build up we feeling. John Dewey said 'Democracy begins with conversation'.

XXIII. Telephonic Conversation

Conversation between two persons over the telephone also is a form of dyadic communication. When compared to dialogue or face-to-face communication, telephonic conversation has certain limitations. The important feature of face-to-face communication, i.e., the use of non-verbal communication in the form of gestures, facial expression, etc. is lost here. But it is one of the easiest, fastest and efficient ways of communication in this technologically advanced world.

1. Points to remember while making and attending calls

Making calls

1. Dial the number correctly. Keep a book with a list of important telephone numbers next to the telephone.

2. Think about what you have to say; if you have to say a number of things helpful to write down the important points. This will save time and money.

Attending Calls

1. Greet the caller, and reveal your identity or the name of the institution, department, office, etc. e.g., Good morning, Global Music Academy.
2. Hold the mouth piece carefully and speak clearly.
3. Find out the identity of the caller.
4. Always keep a note pad and pencil next to the telephone. This will help you to take down messages.
5. Lift the receiver with your left hand, so that you can use your right hand to write.
6. Take down messages clearly and correctly.
7. Be polite even if a wrong number call comes.

2. Some suggestions to converse effectively over the telephone

1. Speak politely and cheerfully. If you are busy when somebody calls for a chat be polite and tactfully say that you are busy at the moment and that you will call back later and keep your promise.
2. Modulate your voice - Unlike in face-to-face conversation, non-verbal communication (facial expression, gestures, etc.) cannot be used in telephonic conversation. Therefore, it is important to modulate your voice in accordance with the theme of the talk.
3. Speak clearly and distinctly.
4. Listen carefully to the caller. Let the caller finish his/her part of the conversation or message and then only reply.

Examples

Example 1

A - Hello. May I speak to Suja, please.

B - Could you tell me who's calling?

A - This is Anila. I am her friend.

B - Hold the line please. I'll check if she is in her office.

B - (After some time) I'm sorry. Ms. Suja is not here at the moment.

Can I take a message?

A - Yes. Could you ask her to give me a call please?

My number is 9895829595.

B - Could you repeat the number please?

A - Of course. It's 9895829595.

B - O.K. I'll surely pass on the message.

A - Thank you. Bye.

B - Bye.

Example 2

David - Hello. Is it 2673032?

John - Yes, it is.

David - Can I talk to Ms. Mary?

John - Sorry, she is not in the office. May I know who is on the line?

David - I am David, a friend of hers. John - Would you like me to convey a message?

David - Yes, Inform her that the interview is scheduled for the 5th of October.

John - I'll make sure that she gets the message.

David - Thank you.

XXIV. Interviews

Interview is a type of face-to-face communication. It can be thought of as an oral questionnaire.

Here, the interviewer asks some questions and the interviewee gives the reply orally. There is a mutual relationship between the interviewer and interviewee, i.e., there is a rapport between the two.

Rapport IR <—> IE Interviewer – Interviewee — The interviewer should be a skilled person for the interview to be a success. With such a skilled interviewer, interview is a good data gathering device. Types of interview I. Based on type of question.

Interview: There are two types of interview. One is structured and another one is unstructured.

1. *Structured interview:* In structured interviews, the questions are prepared beforehand. Here, the interviewer has no choice to change a question, the order is asked or how it is asked. Usually, for data collection purpose structure interview is used.

2. *Unstructured interview:* Here, the interviewer has the freedom to change a question if the situation demands. He can also change the order of questions or spontaneous questions. Counselling interview is of this type. This is usually by trained counsellors.

Q. Depending on the purpose.

Interview

Employment interview. *Data collection interview.*

The purpose of employment interview is for assessing the interviewee, whereas that of data collection interview is for gathering information required by the interviewer.

1. Employment Interview

In order to select candidates for a particular job or position, most of the employers conduct an interview. The interview is a very useful technique which helps the employer to find out whether the applicant is suited for the job. Since it is a face-to-face interaction it has many advantages. A number of important information not revealed in writing can be obtained through an interview.

The attitude, emotion, calibre and many personality traits of applicant can be assessed by this technique. It also gives the applicant an opportunity to get an idea about the working environment and nature of the job.

Suggestions for achieving success while attending an employment interview

Every applicant would like to succeed in an interview. It warrants careful preparation on the part of the applicant to succeed in an interview. The prospective employer seeks candidates who are efficient, committed and suited for the job and he searches for these traits in your personality during the interview.

(i) Physical appearance: The way you dress-certainly tell a lot about your personality. A well-dressed person is sure to create a good impression. Never wear a dress in which you feel uncomfortable. It would make you self-conscious and take away some of your confidence.

(ii) Body language: Your posture, gesture, etc., should radiate confidence. Carry yourself with poise and care but be careful not to appear artificial.

(iii) A good speaking voice: Average speed of speaking, distinct pronounciation, earnestness and sincerity are some essentials for a good speaker.

(iv) Mannerisms: Avoid awkward mannerisms like shaking your knees or feet to and fro while sitting, fidgeting with your handkechief or pen, etc. This will give the impression that you are nervous and not confident.

(v) Attention: Listen to the interviewer attentively and answer only after he finishes the question.

Assessment Record Sheet

Physical Appearance and Social manners

-Dress

-Neatness

-Politeness

Qualification

-Education

-Training

-Experience

Personality

-Sincerity -Leadership -Diplomacy -Perseverance

Intellect

-Knowledge

(Range and Depth) -Memory Power -Potential for Development

Motivation

-Aim -Interest -Attitude -Aptitude

Sociability

-Co-operative -Service minded -Dedicated

Steps for Conducting an Interview

1. Preparation for the Interview

The interviewer should prepare a questioaire in advance. He should decide upon the kind of information to be gathered, the manner in which the results should be recorded, whether the interview should be structured or unstructured, etc.

(i) Conducting the interview

* A good rapport should be established so that the interviewee will feel at ease.
* The interview may be started with a pleasant conversation.
* Ask the questions clearly and give time for the interviewee to answer.
* Listen attentively to the answer.
* Maintain a neutral stance. Don't show surprise, anger, etc., to the response of the subjects.
* Be careful not to suggest answers to questions.

(ii) Recording

The responses should be recorded using appropriate recording devices, so that it can be evaluated later on.

2. Data Collection Interviews

Interview is used also as a technique of data collection. The procedure and manner of conducting the interview is almost the same in both employment interview and data collection interview. The main difference lies in the purpose for which it is conducted. An interview for data collection normally aims at gathering specific information regarding some issue studied, and the information collected should be presented in the form of a report, article, etc. Such information is normally gathered from experts in the particular field concerned.

Points to remember while conducting an interview for data collection

(i) State down the objective of the interview. The type and amount of information that you wish to gather should be clear in your mind.

(ii) Make a frame work for the interview - the questions to be asked, the order of questions, etc., should be decided upon.

(iii) Proper recording devices should be used. If tape recorder is not available, a note-pad and pen should be taken for taking down the important points.

(iv) Note taking should not hinder the natural flow of the interview. Care should be taken to be as unobtrusive as possible while taking down notes.

(v) The data should be recorded accurately. Inaccurate notes will distort the study and may cause confusion.

(vi) Be tactful and attentive. Give the interviewee enough time to answer the question and try not interrupting or arguing with the interviewee. Listen to what the person is saying.

(vii) A pleasant atmosphere should be maintained. This will help in creating a good rapport between the intervewee and interviewer.

(viii) If vague or unclear answers are given ask for clarification. .

(ix) Avoid embarassing or annoying questions.

(x) Last but not the least; be well-prepared for the interview.

Example

Shaheen	-	Excuse me sir.
(Interviewee)	-	Please come in.
Interviewer	-	Good afternoon sir.
Shaheen	-	Good afternoon. Sit down please.
Interviewer	-	Thank you sir.
Shaheen	-	Could you tell me your name please

- I am Shaheen Ahmed.
- O.K. Mr. Shaheen, please introduce yourself.
- Well, as I told you my name is Shaheen Ahmed. I stay at Joseph Road in Calicut. I've done my "post-graduation in Chemistry from the University of Calicut.
- Do you have any working experience?
- Yes sir, I have two years experience as an assistant project officer in the Spices Research Centre.
- You know that ours is a company focussing on cosmetics. How do you think you could help us?
- I am in search of a job which will utilise my ability to the maximum. I am sure I will have ample opportunity in your company to show my talents. My experience in the Spices Research Board will help me in conducting research on how various spices can be used effectively in cosmetic industry.
- Do you think that a product which has compromised on quality will move in the market just because of good advertisement?
- Well, may be in the beginning, but I think it will not last. My opinion is that one should not compromise on the quality of a product, because ultimately it is this factor that will help you to face the tough competition in this field.
- Thank you for sharing your views with us Mr. Shaheen. It was a pleasure talking to you.
- Thank you, sir.

XXV. Language Comprehension and Production

The basic function served by spoken language is to communicate between members of the same language group. It is used for various purposes like face-to-face communication, telephonic conversation, etc. Spoken language is a medium of communication in personal talks as well as at meetings, seminars, conferences and discussions. In meetings, seminars, etc., a number of persons come together to share experiences or to discuss points, concerns or interests. This coming together can be classified based on purposes for which the group meets, the types of participants and communicative pattern.

(a) Conducting Meetings

Many meetings are held now a days. A properly planned and executed meeting can be a very potent instrument to improve organisational and professional communications. The effectiveness of a meeting depends on the extent of preparation that has gone into it.

1. Types of Meetings

Based on purpose, meetings can be classified into different types.

(i) Informative.

* Gather information: For oneself or for colleagues
* Passing on information: Help the group to grasp information.

(ii) Consultative

* *Solving a problem.* A number of possible solutions to a problem are generated and examined.
* *Instructing.* The group is made to apply certain skills or knowledge.
* *Motivating.* Encourage a group to become committed to a particular idea or course of action.
* *Ad hoc.* The group is made to examine a particular issue and give opinion.
* *Persuading.* Negotiate a deal among the members.

iii. Decision-making

Help a group to reach a conclusion or decide on a particular problem. The group activity in the meeting leads to the result or objective for which it is organised. The success of a meeting is indicated by the end results. A positive outcome.

XXV. Techniques of Teaching English

The term technique defined is a classroom activity. Different methods make use of different kinds of classroom activities. "A technique is a particular trick, strategem or contrivance used to accomplish an immediate objective". (Edward Antony, 1963). He further adds, "A technique is implementational—that which actually takes place in a classroom".

Importance of techniques

The aim in any class is to involve all the students all the times. It is only too easy to waste time through imperfect techniques. The term technique can be looked at in two different ways namely classroom techniques and teaching techniques. By classroom technique, we mean the classroom management techniques. Here are a few basic classroom techniques which are not difficult to remember:

1. *Look at all the students in the class.* When you are teaching, look evenly from one side to another. This will help you to have a glimpse of what is going on in the class all the time, and to know who is paying attention and who isn't, so that you can adapt your teaching accordingly.
2. *Vary your techniques of asking questions.* Questions are a way of compelling the attention of your students. If someone is seen not listening ask him a question. However, don't start with the name of the student you are addressing.

Doing this will make the rest of the class inattentive, their interest will be in finding out what that particular student is going to say. Instead, put the question to the whole class. Look around and when everyone is working to find out the answer you can perhaps ask the particular student to answer.

3. *Don't go round the class.* Move around hither and thither and go

back to someone you've just questioned, so that everyone realises he or she may be asked at any time.

4. *Include everyone.* Make sure that everyone is called on equally.
5. *Make sure the class is seated in the best possible way.* Probably, the best arrangement is to have everyone ranged round the wall in a circle. Ideally, everyone should be able to see everyone else so that they can all participate in what is being said.
6. Limit teacher-talking time.
7. Write clearly and legibly because clear black board work is essential.
8. Encourage your students.
10. Be careful in the use of grammatical terms. Encourage your students to practise English outside the classroom—make them read books in English outside the classroom. At the beginning of each lesson—asks the class about the latest news (if possible).
11. Take account of different levels within the class. Ask difficult questions to the brighter ones, and then ask the same questions later to those who lag behind. Make a more advanced student sit next to a less advanced one so that he can help. Do group work where you mix brighter ones with those who know less.
12. Deal with individual problems. It is often best to deal with individual problems after the class.
13. Correct your students systematically—even in the middle of a discussion in English, state the correct phrase of word, while not interrupting the student.

(Adapted from: Some basic classroom techniques —- John Haycraft).

Teaching techniques include questioning techniques and testing techniques also.

XXVII. Teaching Techniques

As mentioned in the introductory paragraph, a technique is a contrivance used to accomplish an immediate objective. As the immediate objectives keep changing, the technique also must be changing. At the same time, a technique or techniques must be consistent with a method—

an overall plan for the orderly presentation of language material, no part of which contradicts, and all of which is based upon, the selected approach (Edward Anthony, 1983). In the following sections you will learn the various techniques.

XXVIII. Teaching Vocabulary

Vocabulary refers to a set of lexemes, including single words, compound words and idioms. Words can be divided into two classes, content words and function words. Content words are words which refer to a thing, quality, state or action and which have meaning when the words are used alone. Content words are mainly nouns, verbs, adjectives, and adverbs. For example, book, run, musical, quickly. Content words are also called lexical words, full words.

Function words are those which have little meaning on their own but which show grammatical relationships in and between sentences (grammatical meaning)—conjunctions, preposition, articles.

For example, — and, to, the—are some function words. Function words are also called form words, empty words, grammatical words, structural words, structure words.

This implies that a vocabulary item or a lexical item can be more than one word. For example, a greeting like 'How do you do? is a complete phrase with a single meaning. Also the word 'how' may suggest that the phrase will be a question but we know that it is not a phrase but a greeting.

In introducing the vocabulary, there is a heed to limit the vocabulary that is introduced. This depends on the list of active vocabulary and passive vocabulary. "Active vocabulary—refers to words which the students understand, can pronounce correctly, and use constructively very often in speaking and writing. Passive vocabulary refers to words that the student recognises and understands when they occur in content but which he cannot produce correctly himself." Also they are words that he does not use frequently. For example, well-educated people may 'know' many thousands of words in the sense that when they hear or read them they face no difficulty in understanding the words. At the same time, the same people probably use only about 2,000 words in a normal daily conversation. In class X, a word like 'accumulate' may be part of a students active vocabulary, but learning more and more vocabulary items does not necessarily increase a person's fluency. Knowing a word is not a simple process. For students to add the word to their active vocabularies they need to know the contexts in which it can occur, the possible and impossible connotations of the word (words it can, or cannot, co-occur with) as well as more connotational meanings of the word. For example, 'little' and 'small' mean the same thing,—most students of English have no difficulty in understanding the sentence, 'which would you like—the big one or the small one?' Even such simple words, however pose difficulties for active use—it is possible to say what a pretty little dress, but not what a pretty small dress.

This implies that in dealing with new words, it is helpful to guide students towards those words which will help them to add to their active vocabularies, and to distinguish these for students from the much larger number of passive items.

The following techniques can be used in teaching vocabulary items:

1. *Explain difference or meaning*: This means that we have to ignore word by word translations for we cannot have a direct equivalent in a language for a word in another language. Also, a language is a system and each word has its meaning defined in relation to other words. So, it is always more helpful to explain the difference in meaning rather than the meaning itself.

Let us take the following example: bush and tree. It is easy, if done visually and contrastively.

If the reader is in any doubt, then try to explain the meaning of 'bush'.

Also note that the student will not be able to master the vocabulary until he understands the difference between them. Hence, a contrastive explanation becomes more helpful in the teaching of vocabulary.

Word-Association

Becoming aware of certain kinds of relationship between one word, and another makes learning simpler for the students. The following are some important relationships:

(i) *Synonyms*- Though words have similar denotative meaning their connotational meanings differ. For example, it will be simpler for the teacher to say very large for the word enormous.

(ii) *Antonyms* - These are often thought of as opposites. It is important to remember that, not hot, for instance, it does not always mean cold. In these cases, students usually start by learning the extremes, and later learn intermediate words: hot - warm - cool - cold.

(iii) *Complements* - Here two words exist, and one word automatically excludes the other — single/married. It is possible to explain by saying 'single' means not married. This idea may be extended to groups of incompatible words like morning-afernmoon-evening-night. Teach such words in groups as the meaning depends directly on the meaning of other words.

(iv) *Converses* - Each pair of words implies the other: parent/child, employer/employee.

(v) *hyponyms:* car, van, bus, lorry are hyponyms of vehicle. Often such words are difficult to handle without translation.

2. (i) *Demonstration:* Certain words like stagger, chuckle can very well be taught by giving a verbal explanation accom-anied by a physical demonstration. The demonstration helps the learner to understand the meaning clearly, and to fix the words in the student's minds.

(ii) Using the real things.

(iii) Drawing or sketching here you need not be artists to make simple sketches which illustrate meaning.

(iv) Using the black board to show grades: Words like orange, (colour), cool may be explained by presenting them with groups of related words.

hot	red	certainly/definitely
warm	orange	probably/possibly
cool	yellow	

(v) *Using antonyms:* It is usually much easier to offer explanations. For example, to teach the word 'rude'—by saying rude means not polite. Also there are a very few exact synonyms within a language, and it is easy to give the wrong impression by, for example, equating little and small. It is also extremely difficult to find a synonym which is enough to help the student. There is little point in simply providing another new word to explain the one the student does not understand.

(vi) *Using synonyms*: Sometimes it is helpful particularly with a relatively unimportant word of passive vocabulary to provide a quick synonym explanation.

(vii) *Using the dictionary:* One technique, for explaining words which teachers too frequently overlook is asking the class whether anybody knows the word—individual students to learn things outside the classroom—and, if not, asking one or more students to look up the word in a dictionary. In this way, the process of learning a new word also provides practice in important learning—skills and in using the dictionary.

(viii) *Giving verbal explanations:* Some language items are the best explained by being used in a variety of contexts with the teacher commenting on the use.

(ix) *Translating*: You should not over use or under-use this technique. When you want to introduce technical words like 'measles' - or words which are 'a kind of...' e.g., oak. The only sensible way to explain is by translation.

4. However, before using 'explanation' as a technique it will be good if you bear in mind the following questions:

(i) Is the word for active use or passive use by the students?

(ii) Is vocabulary studies the main part of the particular classroom activity?

(iii) Is your intention to explain an unexpected difficulty without disturbing the main flow of the lesson?

(iv) Also ask the question, why a particular word is explained at all.

5. *Classroom activities for learning vocabulary:* Vocabulary is best learned when someone feels that a certain word is needed. Hence, the following classroom activities are suggested.

(i) Guessing games in which members of the class are identified by location and by clothing. e.g.,: the boy wears

(ii) Actions that are performed in response to commands —using command cards.

(iii) Drawing of pictures by students to match English description.

(iv) Discussion of pictures drawn by members of the class.

(v) Using aids in the classroom:

(a) Objects already in the classroom.

(b) Objects that can easily be brought to class.

(c) Drawings by the teacher and by students.

(d) Pictures from magazines and newspapers.

(e) Demonstrations to show actions.

6. Presenting an idiom and consolidating it depends essentially on finding a precise context or being able to explain it with equivalents or on being able to give a sufficient number of examples of its use. Let us for example, take the idiomatic phrase, 'on top of the world'. Let's say it appears in a dialogue where someone has just won a lot of money at the races. You introduce the alternatives:

I'm feeling on top of the world

I feel

Context: Explain that he is on top of the world because he has won the race.

Equivalents: very happy, feels wonderful, ecstatic etc.

Examples: Here, you could prompt with simple situations to which the students respond.

(a) He's passed his examination. He's on top of the world.

(ii) She's got a good job. She's on top of the world. Checking: Get your students to produce examples, prompting if necessary. 'The holidays have begun', I've brought a new car' etc. Ask your students to invent sentences in pairs, and then get them to tell the rest of the class. Or, get them to devise little dialogues with variations: 'You must be on top of the world'. Don't you feel on top of the world?

Note: Whenever you present a vocabulary item, check that students have understood, and revise briefly with equivalents and other examples on successive days.

The techniques that a teacher can use for presentiig new vocabulary items can be put in a nutshell as shown below:

1. Deducing the meaning in context.

2. Creating a context (in case you need to teach abstract vocabulary items).
3. Describing or defining.
4. Taking the class out and teaching in a living context.
5. Showing objects.
6. Drawing.
7. Miming.
8. Giving opposite.
9. Giving synonyms.
10. Translating.
11. Showing pictures/flash cards.
12. Using wall charts (for a brief description on these read the lesson on 'Visual Aids').
13. Word games.
14. Using a dictionary.
15. Narrating a parallel story.
16. Using the mother tongue.

To conclude, to know a language is the ability to (i) recognise it in spoken or written form. (ii) recall it at will. (iii) relate it to an appropriate object or concept, (iv) use it in the appropriate grammatical form (v) in speech pronounce, it in a recognisable way, (vi) use it at the appropriate level of formality, (vii) in writing spell it correctly, (viii) use it with words it correctly goes with, and (ix) be aware of its connotations and associations.

XXIX. A Few More Language Teaching Techniques

Cummings Device: This technique is used to practice useful, high, frequency sentences and variations of those sentences. The sentences are always in questions the answer in pairs. This will enable the students to ask and receive simple information. It has a few blanks where the words or/phrases are to be put it. The words and phrases are given separately.

For example., . A: At what time does the bus leave?

B: It leaves at I.

A: Where does it leave from.

B: It leaves from I_.

I	II
Six o'clock	Platform 1
quarter past six	Platform 2
half past six	Platform 3
ten minutes to six etc.	etc.

Procedure in using this technique

(i) The conversation is presented to begin with.

(ii) It must be made sure that the students understand the words.

(iii) The students are asked to repeat after the teacher.

(iv) For example,

Teacher: What does time the bus leave? It leaves at 6 o'clock.

Teacher: Where does it leave from? It leaves from Platform 1.

(v) The students are helped to respond. Here, the teacher can take one part and make the students respond. Later the parts can be changed.

(v) Students are asked to practice the conversation with each other while the teacher listens and makes corrections.

Role-play

This technique is used to put your students into a realistic communication situation. The purpose is to

(i) Sharpen their listening comprehension skills.

(ii) Bring them in contact with the new language, and discover areas where they need additional practice. Usually, the role-play is between the teacher, and one or more students.

It can be a dialogue between a doctor and a patient -(or) a shop-keeper and a customer.

Procedure

(i) The teacher explains the situations.

(ii) He selects the 'cast'. Puts himself in one of the key roles.

(iii) He makes other students take notes.

(iv) He role-plays the situation.

(v) Attempts reconstructing a written version of the role-play.

Construct a log

This technique is used to involve students directly in the language class by giving them the opportunity to write their own dialogues. When the students are writing their material, they may face linguistic problems that will probably stimulate questions and investigations into the language.

The activity can be, writing a dialogue using the given words and phrases. You can tell your students that the dialogue is between a doctor and patient.

Tell them they need not use every word that they find in the list.

Example:

hurt	fever
pain	take a pill
ache	take temperature
headache	give an injection

Procedure

(i) Go over the list of words and phrases with the students to be sure they understand them and have some idea of how to use them. Make each students say a sentence using each word or phrase.

(ii) Make the students work individually or in groups to write the dialogue.

(iii) Check each dialogue. Point out errors and help the students. Don't be harsh.

(iv) Ask them to practice in pairs or groups.

(v) Ask each group to present the dialogue to the rest of the class.

This construct a log technique can be used even without providing the students with any list of words. They can be asked to develop one on their own.

Substitution drill

This technique is used to get a feeling for a particular structure or sentence pattern or grammatical construction by forcing the repetition of the basic sentence while at the same time producing meaningfully different sentences by changing some part of it.

Procedure

The teacher says the basic sentence and adds a word that is to be substituted. The basic sentence is called frame.

The word to be substituted is called cue.

There are different varieties of substitution drills.

In some varieties, the substitution may effect a change in the sentence. In some other varieties, the substitution may be at the level of the word.

Example:

I have a pencil

1. book	2. box
3. pen	4. ball
5. notebook	6. piece of chalk

(This is called a single slot drill.)

Procedure

1. The teacher gives the model and gives only the single word substitution.

Example:

Teacher says	students respond
pencil	I have a pencil
pen	I have a pen.

Note:

1. This can be done in chorus, or individually.
2. The teacher can make one of the students conduct the drill.
3. He can use real objects or flash cards with pictures of the single word.

Expansion drill

This technique is used to give the students opportunity to make more complex sentences. This technique is useful particularly in helping the students to learn how to add modifying words, phrases and clauses.

Procedure

(i) The teacher, through a set of instructions asks the students to add a new element to a basic sentence, and make all the necessary changes that the new elements will cause.

(ii) Makes the student say the sentence.

(iii) Makes the student say the sentence either individually or in groups or in chorus.

Example:

Mr Ramanathan is busy—basic sentence.

Add the word 'often' to the sentence—instruction.

Mr Ramanathan is often busy.

Exercises for the students

(a) We drive to work, (b) Rajesh watches TV

(c) Srilekha speaks English.

An expansion drill is used to.

— Add a frequency word (always, never, sometimes, usually, etc.)

— Add adjectives (big, small)

— Add prepositional phrases (at the bank, in this room, on the floor, etc).

— Add time phrases (in the morning, at noon, today)

— Add a relative construction.

A dialogue is a series of utterance by two or more people. Dialogue can be (a) contrived dialogue (b) directed dialogue (c) model dialogue, and (d) open dialogue.

A contrived dialogue is one which has an abnormally high number of words or structures related to a particular topic.

Directed dialogue, "In methodology, this technique consists of learning the dialogue by heart, where the teacher suggests exactly what the students should say in both questions and answers. The dialogue should be over learned to the point of automatic response to the dialogue situation and practised in various adoptions. However, it should be noted that there is a limit to the amount of repetition that is effective, even with reinforcement, such as praise", remarks Wilga Rivers (1964).

A model dialogue is used at the repetition stage of a lesson. Open dialogues are used for oral practice where the learner must complete his half of the dialogue by listening carefully to each stimulus.

Action chain

It is a technique that can be used to teach the primary students to get them to write 5-6 connected sentences at a time. The teacher prepares the students orally before asking them to write.

Example:

"Rajesh, go near the black board. Take a piece of chalk. Draw a line on the board. Draw another line above it. Rubd off those lines. Come back to your seat."

After these actions are performed pupils may be asked to write six sentences in the past tense. An extension of the 'action chain' is getting the pupils to do simple experiments. This technique is used for practising several pronoun forms and several verb tenses all in one sequence. These actions must be done deliberately so that the students' verbal and physical responses are co-ordinated, and this technique helps in both introducing and practising action verbs.

Index